BURST

Topics for Today's Teens

WORLD RELIGIONS

Danny Rhodes

09 10 11 12 13 14 15 16 17 — 10 9 8 7 6 5 4 3 2 1

Editor: Josh Tinley
Production Editor: Pam Shepherd
Design Manager: Keely Moore
Cover Design: Keely Moore

CONTENTS

About BURST: WORLD RELIGIONS

Why World Religions?

During his 2009 inauguration President Barack Obama said, "We are a nation of Christians and Muslims, Jews and Hindus, and nonbelievers. We are shaped by every language and culture, drawn from every end of this earth." He added, "We know that our patchwork heritage is a strength, not a weakness."

This was the first time that an American president referenced such a diversity of religions in an inauguration speech, and he did so for good reason. Our country is more diverse in its religious makeup than it has ever been in its short history. While Christians remain the overwhelming majority of religious people in the United States, we are increasingly aware of religious diversity, both in the U.S. and throughout the world.

Youth are especially aware of the diversity of faith traditions here and around the world. Many Christian youth have friends, classmates, or neighbors who are Jewish, Muslim, Buddhist, or Hindu; many have attended bar and bat mitzvahs or have some knowledge of the holidays and customs observed by their friends of other faiths.

Today's youth also have more access to information and ideas about God, religion, and specific faith traditions than any other generation in history. Unfortunately, with all the information that is available on the Internet and through media such as cable television, it can be difficult to know what is accurate and reliable and what is a stereotype or a distortion.

The purpose of this resource is to help Christian youth better understand the religious beliefs and traditions of their Hindu, Buddhist, Jewish, and Muslim friends, peers, and neighbors and be better equipped to process all of the ideas and information they encounter.

What Will Youth Learn From This?

The most important lesson that youth can learn from this study is that all four of the faith traditions they will explore—Hinduism, Buddhism, Judaism, and Islam—are ancient, diverse, and complex. Like Christianity, each of these faiths is divided into several branches or denominations, each of which has its own story and core emphases. What is true for one Hindu is not necessarily true for all Hindus, and the same can be said about Buddhists, Jews, and Muslims (and Christians). In other words it is impossible to do any of these religions justice in a one- or two-hour youth group session, and it would be easy to leave youth with a distorted view of these traditions. Thus this resource sticks to the essentials, giving youth a very basic overview of these four faiths and introducing them to some of the core beliefs, traditions, and practices that most of the adherents of each of these religions have in common.

The hope of BURST: WORLD RELIGIONS is that your youth will come away from this study with:

- a (very) basic knowledge of the origins, history, and sacred writings of Hindusim, Buddhism, Judaism, and Islam;

- a (very) basic understanding of the beliefs, practices, and traditions of these four faith traditions;

- an awareness of some of the stereotypes and common misconceptions about each of these four faith traditions;

- definitions of several key terms and concepts related to each faith tradition;

- an interest in learning more about each of these faith traditions;

- a richer appreciation and deeper understanding of their personal Christian faith.

How Do I Use This Resource?

This study is divided into five sessions: (1) Hinduism; (2) Buddhism; (3) Judaism; (4) Islam; and (5) Bringing It All Together.

These sessions were designed with Sunday evening or mid-week youth fellowship in mind, but could also work in the context of a Sunday school class or small-group Bible study. Each of the first four sessions begins with a six-page article for you, the leader. The purpose of these articles is to equip you to answer some basic questions about Hinduism, Buddhism, Judaism, or Islam.

Each of these sessions also includes the following learning activities:

- **Whaddaya Know (or Think You Know)?:** This activity invites youth to name all the information they know (or think they know) about each religion and to pose any questions they have.

- **The Truth Is Out There:** In this true-or-false activity, youth will confront some stereotypes and common misconceptions about each faith tradition.

- **Dialogue With an Expert:** Each session recommends inviting an expert on the religion you will be studying. This expert could be a leader from a nearby temple, synagogue, or mosque; a professor from a nearby university; or simply someone in your community who is a practicing Hindu, Buddhist, Jew, or Muslim and can give your youth a sense of how his or her faith influences his or her day-to-day life.

- **Word Up:** In this activity, youth will attempt to match important terms and concepts related to each religion to the correct definitions or descriptions.

- **Sending Forth:** This closing activity gives the youth an opportunity to reflect on their Christian faith in light of what they have learned about other traditions. (For example, the "Sending Forth" activity in the Islam session

The Golden Rule

The introduction to each religion begins with an example of what we know as the Golden Rule from one of that religion's sacred texts. While the world's major religions differ in significant ways, they all affirm that we should treat others as we would like to be treated. A longer list of examples of the Golden Rule from the world's faith traditions is available at *burst.abingdonyouth.com.*

Burst: World Religions

reviews the Five Pillars of Islam—which instructs Muslims in how to live faithful lives—and challenges the youth to think of some of the "pillars" of Christianity, or actions that Christians take in response to God's grace.)

BURST: WORLD RELIGIONS also includes a **student book.** This 24-page, full-color booklet, which comes in packs of five, provides key information about Hinduism, Buddhism, Judaism, and Islam, along with a list of additional resources. The student book does not include written activities and is not required for any of the sessions (though you may find it helpful when reviewing concepts such as The Eightfold Path or when comparing the Jewish Tanak to the Christian Old Testament). It does act as a reference and a reminder of what the youth have learned during your time together. Give a student book to each youth during the first session he or she attends.

How Do I Prepare for Each Session?

Prior to each session, read the introductory article (the first six pages of Chapters 1–4) to learn more about the faith tradition you will be exploring. Record any questions you have, and do your best to address these questions, either by referring to some of the resources listed on pages 79–80 or at *burst.abingdonyouth.com* or by talking to someone who belongs to that particular faith tradition. Be prepared to answer basic questions about each religion, but also approach each session with an awareness of what you aren't sure about or what you don't know. When in doubt, refer youth to a reliable book, person, or website that can answer their questions. (Some relevant books and websites are listed on pages 79–80. A list of web resources is also included on page 24 of the student book.)

In the interest of engaging multiple senses and different learning styles, each session includes food and music suggestions. The food suggestions consist of meals or snacks that are common among practitioners of each faith tradition and that adhere to that religion's dietary regulations. The music provides examples of ways in which some practitioners of each religion express their faith.

Activities to Get You Started

Here are a few activities to introduce the subject of world religions.

The Truth Is Out There

The purpose of this activity is to make youth aware of the misconceptions that people have about other faith traditions by looking at some of the misconceptions that people have about Christianity.

You will need: a markerboard and markers.

Ahead of time list on a markerboard the following statements about Christianity, which may be true or false. (Actually they are all false, but the youth shouldn't know that beforehand.)

> **1. Christians are polytheists who worship three gods.**
>
> **2. Christians are cannibals who eat human flesh and drink human blood.**
>
> **3. Christians believe that God rewards people who do good things and punishes people who do bad things.**
>
> **4. Christianity is all about following a bunch of rules included in the Bible.**
>
> **5. All Americans are Christians.**

For each statement ask the youth to vote "true" or "false." The answers are: 1. *False—a misunderstanding of the Trinity has given many people throughout history the incorrect impression that Christians worship three gods;* 2. *False—when early Christians spoke of eating the body and drinking the blood of Christ, some people incorrectly assumed that they were cannibals;* 3. *False—Christians believe that all people are sinners and that salvation comes from God's grace;* 4. *False—for Christians, a relationship with Christ is more important than any list of rules;* 5. *False—while the majority of Americans profess the Christian faith, the United States is also home to millions of Jews, Muslims, Buddhists, Hindus, and nonbelievers.*

Say: "Some of these statements probably sounded absurd, but they are actual misconceptions that people have (or have had) about Christianity. Chances are that we, as Christians, have similar misconceptions about other faith traditions. Each week, as we explore a different religion, we'll look at some of those misconceptions."

Around the World

Post a world map on the wall in your meeting space. (If possible, use a map that is blank except for the boundaries of the countries; see *burst.abingdonyouth.com* for links to websites that provide blank maps for classroom use.) Using information from the Internet or from books on the subject (again, see the website for suggested resources), color in the map to show where the

> **You will need:** a map (or maps) of the world and markers or colored pencils.

different major religions are most prominent. Challenge the youth to use stripes or color combinations to indicate where multiple religions are prominent. (For example, youth might use blue to represent Christianity and red to represent Islam; places where both Christianity and Islam are common could be colored in purple or in red and blue stripes.)

Option: Instead of coloring a single map, hand out copies and allow youth to color in the maps individually or in groups. You could also do a progressive map, adding the color for each religion during the session you study that particular religion.

Movie Night

Before beginning your series on world religions, gather to watch the 1992 film *Baraka*. It is a stunning documentary (without narration) about contrasting ways of life and contains footage of forms of worship that

> **You will need:** the film *Baraka* on DVD.

represent all of the faith traditions included in this study. You might also review clips from the movie during each of the sessions as a visual illustration of some of the traditions and practices you'll be studying. (See the note about video viewing on page 79.)

HINDUISM

This is the sum of duty: do not do to others what would cause pain if done to you.
—*Mahabharata 5:1517*

Introduction

In some regards Hinduism is the most difficult to discuss of the four religions outlined in this study. Because its origins are believed to predate written history, the earliest Hindu beliefs and practices were passed along orally. This oral transmission of knowledge and tradition is responsible for innumerable variations, omissions, and additions that make impossible a clear and unified understanding of the Hindu tradition. Hinduism also has shared time and place with many other religious traditions, including Buddhism, Jainism, Islam, and Sikhism. This exposure has had such an effect on Hinduism that it is often more appropriate to talk about the many "Hindu traditions" that now belong under the umbrella of "Hinduism."

Imagine an acorn that grows into a mighty oak tree. It begins as a singular stem and leaf. Yet over time, and with exposure to the elements of sun, wind, and rain, it does not continue to grow just straight up; it branches off and grows in numerous directions until it becomes a massive umbrella of "tree-ness." However wide the umbrella, the trunk of the tree still begins straight and winds its way up, connecting all of the many branches. But before we can ever swing from its boughs, we must first climb the base. So we now turn to the beginning, or base, of "Hindu-ness."

The Story of Hinduism

Sometime during the third millennium B.C., a traveling group of people known as Aryans migrated into an area of northern India and settled among indigenous people of the Indus Valley region. The Aryans introduced into the region the belief and practice of *rita* (RIT-uh), ritualistic sacrifice of grains and animals to appease various deities and maintain the moral order of the universe. This era of Aryan influence in India is known as the Vedic period, named for the

Vedas, which were a collection of hymns written to the gods. Over time the Aryans began to synthesize many of the beliefs and practices of the indigenous Indic people, including the practice of asceticism—a spiritual retreat that involved long periods of silence, meditation, and restriction of basic needs. This combination of ritual and spirituality ushered in a faith that centered on the belief of *samsâra* (suhm-SAHR-uh): the cycle of birth, life, death, and rebirth through which every soul travels until it finds release, or *moksha* (MOHK-shuh). It was during this era that the practices of yoga and the defining doctrine of karma were established.

By approximately 300 B.C., while continuing to grow, Hinduism had incorporated aspects of other south Asian traditions such as Jainism and Buddhism. This era of Classical Hinduism saw the establishment of Hindu monasteries, practices of vegetarianism and nonviolence, and the development of *jati* (JAH-tee), or "*castes*," social classes determined by heredity. Also, a new set of texts emerged during Classical Hinduism that told stories about and praised a variety of deities. These stories were called *puranas* (puh-RAH-nuhs) and specified how one could show great loyalty and faith, or *bhakti* (BUK-tee), to deities.

What Hindus Believe

It has already been suggested that Hinduism is perhaps the most diverse of all world religions in terms of beliefs and practices. This diversity is created by a general openness to, tolerance for, and acceptance of opposing views. This pluralism and openness is common to all Hindu traditions.

Many Hindus, if asked to define *Hinduism*, would answer "Varnâshrama Dharma," or the teaching of castes and stages in life

A Note on Dates

Since this book is intended for use in Christian communities, all dates are based on the Christian calendar and are written using the abbreviations B.C. (before Christ) and A.D. (anno domini, the year of our Lord). Many adherents of the faith traditions in this study base their dates on other calendars (such as the Hebrew Calendar or the Islamic Calendar) and, when using the Christian calendar, use the abbreviations B.C.E. (before the common era) and C.E. (common era).

that are shared throughout Hinduism. In a manner appropriate to each caste, a person must travel through four stages in life. First, the "student" commits to memorizing the Vedas and studying areas of astrology, science, and the arts. The student then becomes a "householder" by marrying, having children, and following the customary rites (to be discussed more later). After a couple has grown old and their children have begun their separate lives, the husband and wife become "forest dwellers" by retreating from social obligations and devoting themselves to meditation. Finally, by renouncing all worldly possessions and connections, Hindus become "homeless wanderers" and, in anticipation of the realization of *moksha* (salvation through release from the cycle of samsâra), commit their remaining days to yoga practices and pilgrimages to holy sites.

Because Hinduism is considered the world's oldest religion, it has shared time and place with virtually every other religious tradition in human history.

Another common path toward moksha is the devotion to and veneration of gods. The Hindu understanding of god is complicated. In one sense Hindus believe in a single god: Brahman, the ultimate reality and source of all being. On the other hand, some Hindu texts claim the existence of as many as 330 million deities. These many gods are all different manifestations of Brahman. The three primary gods are Brahma, Shiva, and Vishnu; other important deities include Parvati, Lakshmi, Saraswati, and Ganesh. A Hindu develops a relationship with one of these lesser deities because Brahman is impersonal and unknowable. A relationship with a god through study, devotion, offerings, worship, and self-giving establishes a channel through which the deity can bring the devotee closer to moksha. A short list of some of the most popular deities is included on pages 20–21.

One important doctrine in the Hindu traditions that is familiar to many non-Hindus is *karma.* For the Hindu, karma is the guiding force of the universe. How one acts in the present life will affect one's status in the next life. Accumulating good karma through observing rituals, devotion to a deity, and studying the sacred texts can result in one being reborn in a higher caste, thereby progressing along the path toward release from samsâra (cycle of reincarnation).

Likewise, failure to observe the appropriate rituals and practices, and immoral actions in general, can result in bad karmic retribution and lead to rebirth in a lower caste or even a lower form of creation.

Hinduism is also responsible for introducing the world to *yoga*—disciplines that help a person to focus and that elevate the mind to a higher state of consciousness. There are four types of yoga in the Hindu tradition: (1) *Jnana yoga* is the practice of meditation to sharpen the intellect; (2) *Bhakti yoga* involves directing love toward Brahman through devotion and adoration; (3) *Karma yoga* involves doing good deeds for others without expecting anything in return; (4) *Raja yoga* incorporates the other three yogas and addresses the body, mind, and emotions. *Hatha yoga* (a part of raja yoga) disciplines the body and is the most popular form of yoga among non-Hindus.

Hindu Sacred Texts

All of the previously mentioned beliefs were generated or propagated by the sacred texts, or canons, that evolved throughout Hindu history. And there are many sacred texts that Hindus of varying traditions use, but several are universal. The Vedas are considered the earliest of these sacred texts, with the oldest, Rig Veda, dating back to 1500 B.C.E. The Upanishads (oo-PAHN-ih-shahds or yoo-PAN-uh-shads) are philosophical reflections that later were added to the Vedas and which introduced the concept that there is one ultimate reality, Brahman or "God," from which the entire universe was created. Since all of creation was begotten from Brahman, then every living creature also contains a part of God: the *âtman* (AHT-muhn) or "soul." The Upanishads also introduced the idea that, by engaging in yoga practices, one is able to focus bodily energy, in concert with the soul, in an attempt to reach moksha.

Other important texts shared by all strands of Hinduism include the puranas; the Dharmashastras, law books which prescribe the four main castes; and the epics of Mahabharata and Ramayana, which tell of great battles between Aryan and non-Aryan clans. The Bhagavad Gita is a portion of the Dharmashastras that many Hindus consider to be their most sacred scripture. It is a poem that recounts a conversation between the god Krishna (an incarnation of the god

Vishnu) and Arjuna (AR-juh-nuh), a Hindu knight, about how one may attain salvation through obedience to one's caste, practices of asceticism and meditation, devotion to the gods, and observance of ritual.

Hindu Rituals and Festivals

A person's present life and *dharma* (righteous duty) are of the utmost importance to salvation. Therefore those stages of life that all Hindus experience are considered sacrosanct and should be observed by karma-producing rituals called *samskaras*. These ritual celebrations mark all stages of life, including birth, coming of age, marriage, and death.

Another sacred ritual for most Hindus is *darshan*, concentrated eye contact with the sacred. Hindus practice darshan by gazing at a spiritual teacher, or guru; images of deities; sacred objects; or holy sites. For this reason pilgrimages to divine places, such as the Ganges River, the Himalaya Mountains, and holy temples, are important to many Hindus.

Finally, throughout the year Hindus participate in several festivals, or *utsavas,* that not only are fun and entertaining but that also provide opportunities to receive good karma. Festival occasions include Diwali, a festival of lights celebrated in the fall; Holi, a playful and boisterous spring celebration during which rules involving caste and gender are suspended; and Gai Jatra, a festival honoring the cow. In Hinduism, a cow is considered sacred as a symbol of life and a source of important resources such as milk, cheese, butter, and fertilizer.

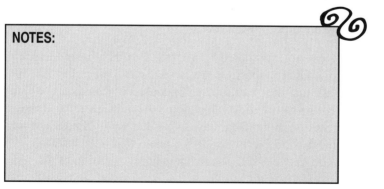

NOTES:

In this Session

Youth should come away from this session with a very basic understanding of Hindu history, beliefs, sacred texts, and practices. In particular, youth should learn the following terms and concepts:

samsâra (suhm-SAHR-uh): the cycle of birth, death, and rebirth that Hindus seek to escape

Brahman (BRAH-muhn): the ultimate reality, the divine grounds of all being

moksha (MOHK-sha): salvation, or release from samsara and oneness with Brahman

karma: literally means "work" or "action." It often refers to the idea that our actions in this life affect the next life: One who does good works will be rewarded; one who does evil will bear the burden of his or her evil.

yogas: spiritual practices that include knowledge, devotion and service to a deity, good works, and contemplation

jati (JAH-tee): a caste, or social class, into which one is born. Good karma results in one being born into a higher caste in the next life.

Youth also should come away from this session knowing the names and basic descriptions of important Hindu deities and sacred texts.

Emphasize that Hinduism is an ancient, diverse, and complex faith and that this session covers only some of the basics.

Getting Ready

As you prepare for this session, read the information about Hinduism on pages 10–15. If you have questions, additional resources are listed on pages 79–80 and at *burst.abingdonyouth.com.*

Keep in mind that Hinduism, like all of the faith traditions included in this study, is an ancient and diverse faith practiced by millions of people. This program will cover only the basic beliefs and practices that are true for most Hindus. Encourage your youth to refrain from drawing conclusions or making assumptions based on limited information. If students would like to learn more, point them to the additional resources on pages 79–80 and at *burst.abingdonyouth.com* and encourage them to seek out and talk to a practicing Hindu.

If possible, invite a Hindu person from your community to talk about Hindu beliefs and practices and to answer any questions the youth may have. (See "Dialogue With an Expert" on page 19.)

✨ Food Ideas

Because the vast majority of the world's Hindu population lives in India, serve Indian cuisine. You could order food from a nearby Indian restaurant or draw from the wealth of Indian cuisine websites on the Internet. If you try your hand at cooking Indian dishes, consider preparing foods that are specific to Hindu festivals such as Diwali (a festival of lights) or Navratri (a nine-night festival of worship and dance).

✨ Music Ideas

Bhajans (BUHJ-uhns), simple Hindu devotional songs that express love for the divine, are widely available on Internet music stores, both on CD and as downloadable MP3s. Consider playing some of these songs in the background as you discuss Hinduism.

Getting Ready: Read the article on pages 10–15 to help you answer basic questions about Hinduism. Also review the following activities and gather or prepare needed supplies.

ACTIVITIES	SUPPLIES
❧ **Whaddaya Know (or Think You Know)? (10 minutes)**	**Sticky notes, pens or pencils**
❧ **The Truth Is Out There (5–10 minutes)** **Preparation:** Write statements at top of page 19 on a markerboard.	**Markerboard, markers**
❧ **Dialogue With an Expert (15–20 minutes)** **Preparation:** Invite a guest expert on Hinduism.	
❧ **Diety ID (10 minutes)** **Preparation:** Collect images of Hindu deities; print descriptions of deities on slips of paper or notecards.	**Pictures of Hindu deities, small slips of paper or notecards**
❧ **Start Over (15 minutes)** **Preparation:** Collect building materials.	**Wooden blocks or plastic cups**
❧ **Word Up (10–15 minutes)** **Preparation:** Print copies of the Word Up: Hinduism worksheet.	**Word Up: Hinduism worksheet, pens or pencils**
❧ **Sending Forth (5–10 minutes)**	**Candle, matches or lighter**

Don't Forget to . . .

Whaddaya Know (or Think You Know)?

To begin, set out sticky notes and pens. Invite the youth to write on the sticky notes information they know (or think they know) about Hinduism. Youth may also write questions they have about Hinduism. Ask them to stick their notes on a markerboard or a designated wall space.

> **You will need:**
> sticky notes and pens or pencils; if you've invited a guest expert, ask him or her to help with this activity.

When everyone has had an opportunity to contribute information and questions, ask the youth to organize the sticky notes. First, ask them to set aside the questions. Then ask them to work together to arrange the remaining stickies into three categories: 1) pretty sure it's true; 2) think it might be true; and 3) not sure if it's true.

If you have invited a Hindu person to speak to your group (see "Dialogue With an Expert" on page 19), ask him or her to review the sticky notes and indicate which statements are true, which are true for some Hindus but not others, which are partially true, and which are completely false.

If you do not have a visiting expert, verify as many of the facts and answer as many questions as possible using the information on pages 10–15 (see also below, "The Truth Is Out There").

Ask the youth to call out Christian denominations and traditions (*United Methodist, Baptist, Lutheran, Roman Catholic, Orthodox, and so on*). Also ask them to think of issues about which Christians disagree (*when and how to baptize, styles of worship, interpretation of Scripture, and so on*). Say: "Like Christianity, Hinduism is a very diverse faith, and what is true for one Hindu might not be true for all Hindus. So today we're going to focus on the essentials: the beliefs and practices that most Hindus have in common."

The Truth Is Out There

List on a markerboard the following common statements about Hinduism, some which are true and some of which are false:

> **You will need:**
> markerboard and markers.

1. **Hindus believe that one's soul, or âtman, moves from one body to the next at rebirth.**

2. **All Hindus are vegetarians.**

3. **Hindus are required to wear a red dot (Bindi) on their foreheads at all times.**

4. **Hot Yoga is a Hindu religious practice**.

For each statement, ask the youth to vote "true" or "false." The answers are: 1. *True;* 2. *False—though Hindus believe that the cow is sacred, and many choose to be vegetarians;* 3. *False—many Hindus wear the "Bindi," but it is not required;* 4. *False—yoga is a Hindu religious practice, but Hot Yoga is a western exercise trend.*

Dialogue With an Expert

If possible, invite a Hindu person from your community to explain the basics of his or her faith and to answer any questions youth may have (such as those the youth wrote on the sticky notes).

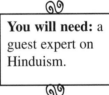

You will need: a guest expert on Hinduism.

Visit *burst.abingdonyouth.com* for a list of Hindu temples in the United States. If there is not a temple in your community, check the faculty of a nearby university for an expert on Hinduism. If your guest requests a list of topics to cover, provide the list of terms and concepts on page 15.

Deity I.D.

Provide images of each of the Hindu deities listed on pages 20–21. Reproducible pictures of these gods are available on pages 76–78 of this book. Links to high-quality, full-color images are available at *burst.abingdonyouth.com.* You might also check your local library for books that include images of these deities. Also provide descriptions, on notecards or slips

You will need: printed pictures, notecards or slips of paper with descriptions of the deities listed on pages 20–21.

of paper, for each of the deities. You can copy these descriptions from pages 20–21 or print them from *burst.abingdonyouth.com*.

Say: "The Hindu understanding of God is complicated. In one sense, Hindus believe in a single god, Brahman, the ultimate reality and source of all being. On the other hand, some Hindu texts claim the existence of as many as 330 million deities. These many gods are all different manifestations of Brahman. A Hindu's task is to identify with one god who can help him or her grow spiritually. Let's take a look at some of the better-known Hindu deities."

Set out the images and descriptions of the gods and challenge the youth to match the images to the descriptions. Allow the youth to work together as one group or divide them into teams to compete for the most correct matches. Give them several minutes to work, then review the answers. (If you divided the youth into teams, consider giving a small prize to the team with the most correct answers.)

The deities and descriptions are:

Brahma: the creator of the universe and one of the three primary Hindu gods. He represents wisdom and knowledge, particularly the wisdom and knowledge of the four Vedas (ancient sacred texts). He also symbolizes the four cardinal directions (north, south, east, and west) and the four aspects of human personality (mind, intellect, ego, and self). His consort (wife) is Saraswati.

Vishnu: one of the three primary Hindu gods. He is the preserver and sustainer of the universe and is believed to have appeared on earth in the form of several avatars, or incarnations. Hindus universally recognize ten avatars of Vishnu, including **Krishna** and **Rama**. Krishna calls for souls to awaken to love and is the teacher of the Bhagavad Gita, one of the most sacred Hindu texts. Rama is a warrior and protector and is considered the ideal man, king, brother, and husband. Vishnu's consort is Lakshmi.

Shiva: one of the three primary Hindu gods. He is the destroyer of the universe; in particular, he destroys sin and ignorance. Shiva usually appears in a meditating posture. His consort is Parvati.

Lakshmi: the goddess of prosperity and generosity (represented by gold coins) and of purity (represented by a lotus blossom). Lakshmi is Vishnu's consort.

Saraswati: the goddess of wisdom and learning who is worshiped mostly by students, teachers, and scholars. She is a musician who plays the music of love and life. Saraswati is the consort of Brahma.

Parvati: the Divine Mother and the goddess who preserves moral order and righteousness. Parvati is considered charming and pleasant but also has a darker side, taking the form of the warrior goddess **Durga** (often depicted riding an animal) or the destroyer goddess **Kali**. Parvati is Shiva's consort.

Ganesh: the first son of Shiva and Parvati. His large head and ears symbolize wisdom and the need to listen to others.

Images and descriptions of the three primary gods—Brahma, Vishnu, and Shiva are found on page 7 of the student book.

Start Over

Assign youth to teams of three or four. Give each team a supply of building materials, such as wooden blocks or plastic cups, and ask each to build a tower. Decide on certain criteria that all of the towers must meet (such as height, shape, symmetry, or color scheme), but don't reveal these criteria to the teams. Walk among the teams as they build and, if a tower doesn't meet your secret crtieria, knock it down and tell that team to start over.

> **You will need:** building materials such as wooden blocks or plastic cups.

After several minutes, reveal your criteria. Ask if any of the teams guessed your criteria and discuss the teams' frustration when they had to begin again.

Say: "This activity is similar to the Hindu concept of samsâra, which is the cycle of birth, life, death, and rebirth. Many Hindus believe that every soul begins in a very simple lifeform."

Ask the youth if they are familiar with the concept of *karma* and explain karma using the information on pages 12–13. Say: "By building good karma, the soul is born into greater and greater lifeforms until finally it is born into a human being. The soul starts out as a human in the lowest social class, or caste or *jati* (JAH-tee), but through good karma, devotion to a deity, and spiritual practices known as yoga, the soul is reborn into higher castes." (If time permits, you might talk more about castes.) After several lives and starting over several times, the soul eventually breaks free from samsâra and becomes one with Brahman. This release from samsâra is called *moksha*."

Word Up

Ask the youth what they know about yoga. Allow for several responses, then review yoga using the information on pages 12–13. Say: "While some forms of yoga are popular among non-Hindus in the United States, yoga is a very important part of the Hindu faith. Let's look now at some other important Hindu terms and concepts."

> **You will need:** copies of the Word Up: Hinduism worksheet, and pens or pencils.

Hand out copies of the Word Up worksheet. This handout is available at *burst.abingdonyouth.com*. Challenge youth, working individually or in teams, to match the terms to their correct definitions. (Some of these terms are defined on page 5 of the student book.) The answers are:

âtman (AHT-muhn): the soul, or part of God that is in every living being

Bhagavad Gita: a sacred poem that recounts a conversation between the god Krishna and Arjuna (AR-juh-nuh), a Hindu knight, about the ethics of killing and how one may attain salvation

Brahman: the one supreme, all-pervading Spirit or God from whom it is believed that all creation was developed

Brahmin: a member of the highest priestly caste

guru: a teacher of religious knowledge or spiritual insight

jati (JAH-tee): a caste, or social class, into which one is born. Good karma results in one being born into a higher caste in the next life.

karma: literally means "work" or "action"; often refers to the idea that our actions in this life affect the next life: One who does good works will be rewarded; one who does evil will bear the burden of his or her evil.

moksha (MOHK-sha): salvation, or release from samsâra and oneness with Brahman

namaste: an outward hand sign that represents spiritual reality and is a greeting. It is performed by placing the palms together in front of the chest and making a slight bow.

samsâra (suhm-SAHR-uh): the cycle of birth, death, and rebirth that Hindus seek to escape

Vedas: collections of hymns written to the gods and the earliest Hindu sacred writings

yogas: spiritual practices that include knowledge, devotion and service to a deity, good works, and contemplation

Sending Forth

Gather the youth in a circle, dim the lights, and light a candle. Say: "Today we learned about some of the basics and essentials of Hinduism. To close, I want you to think about some of the basics of Christianity. If someone who knew little about Christianity asked you to explain your faith, what would you say?"

> **You will need:** a candle and matches or lighter.

Pass around the candle. Invite each person, while holding the candle, to name one thing he or she learned about Hinduism and one basic belief or practice of Christianity. Close in prayer, thanking God for the opportunity to gather as Christians to learn about Hinduism.

BUDDHISM

*Hurt not others in ways that you
yourself would find hurtful.*
—Udana Varga 5:18

Introduction

The Story of Buddhism

In 563 B.C. a child was born to a king who ruled the area now known as Nepal. The king and his family were part of the privileged warrior caste in India. According to legend the king called on fortunetellers to predict the future of his son. They agreed that the child would grow up to fulfill one of two roles: He would live into his caste, be a great warrior who unified India and become a world conqueror—or he would forsake his caste and become a great ascetic and world redeemer. The king named his child Siddhartha Gautama (meaning "the one who attains the goal") and vowed to shelter him from suffering, ensuring that he would live into his destiny as a king.

Siddhartha grew up surrounded by every available princely luxury. He lived in grand palaces, was trained in the martial arts, and was sheltered from the pain and ugliness of humanity. He married and had a son with the princess of a neighboring province. Siddhartha Gautama seemed to be living the perfect life and on his way to becoming a world conqueror.

Life changed for Siddhartha when he decided to take a ride in the forest beyond the palace walls. Despite his father's attempts to clear the riding path of any signs of human suffering, Siddhartha came across an old man on the side of the road. It was his first encounter with aging. The next day while riding again, Siddhartha discovered a sick man. It was his first encounter with illness. On a third day he came across a dead man. It was his first encounter with death. Finally, on a forth ride, Siddhartha came across a Hindu monk holding a bowl for receiving alms. With this encounter, he learned about a simpler way of life that involved withdrawal from the world. These experiences, known as The Four Passing Sights, set Siddhartha down a different path and toward his destiny as a world redeemer.

At age 29, Siddhartha left his family and possessions and fled into the forest in search of enlightenment. First he studied with a Hindu Master to learn deep meditation techniques and the depth of the Hindu religion. Not yet satisfied, he studied with a guru (teacher) who taught him right concentration so as to achieve a trance-like state. Still unfulfilled, Siddhartha joined a group of extreme ascetics who sought enlightenment through bodily depravation. But after several years of denying himself, he found that this deprivation had brought him no closer to his goal. Frustrated, Siddhartha realized that the path to enlightenment could not be found in the extremes of asceticism or abundance, restriction or indulgence. He knew that surely there was a middle way. Resting next to a river beneath a ficus tree (later to be called the Bo or Bodhi tree, meaning "enlightenment"), Siddhartha vowed he would not move until he either reached enlightenment or died.

Today Buddhism is one of the five largest religions in the world.

During this time of deep meditation, the evil spirit Mara visited Siddhartha and tried to break his concentration by offering escape through various temptations and death. But Siddhartha had so emptied himself of ego and desire that Mara could not penetrate his will. Siddhartha reached out with his right hand and touched the ground. At that moment the earth shook, all of the lotus blossoms bloomed on every tree, and the river swelled and washed away the evil spirit. Now free from temptation, Siddhartha gained insight that allowed him to abandon all selfish desire and ignorance. At this moment, called "The Great Awakening," Siddhartha Gautama became the Buddha or "Enlightened One."

For the next forty-five years the Buddha walked across India preaching his message of selflessness. He founded an order of monks who became disciples and practiced and shared Buddha's teachings with others. Buddha continued his ministry and practice of meditation until, at age 80, he died of accidental food poisoning.

Buddhism spread across India and into China, Japan, and Southeast Asia—areas now known as Myanmar, Thailand, and Vietnam. Today it is one of the five largest religions in the world.

What Buddhists Believe

Buddhism shares the Hindu belief that all living things are trapped in *samsâra,* a cycle of rebirth after death or reincarnation. Liberation from this cycle is called *nirvana,* a state of ultimate rest and peace.

The Eightfold Path

- Right views: understanding suffering and the Four Noble Truths

- Right intent: aspiring to get rid of worldly desires, to do good, and to do no harm

- Right speech: avoiding lying, insults, and gossip

- Right action: doing good and not doing harm

- Right livelihood: having an occupation that is not harmful

- Right effort: making an effort to do good in word and action

- Right mindfulness: keeping one's mind alert

- Right concentration: practicing advanced meditation

The Buddha outlined "The Four Noble Truths," which explained the condition of human suffering and how to overcome it. The first Noble Truth is that "All life includes suffering (*dukkha*)." The Buddha believed suffering was the result of everyday experiences such as the pain of birth, fear of death, illness, and separation from love. All of these events are inevitable but can be combatted with compassion and kindness. The second Noble Truth claims that "The cause of suffering is desire." Because people often want things they cannot have or do not need, suffering and disappointment thrive. Thus it is better to live a life of detachment and simplicity, leading to the third and fourth Noble Truths: "Overcoming desire removes suffering," and "Desire is overcome by following the Eightfold Path" (see box).

Correct understanding of the Noble Truths and practice of the Eightfold Path are not a source of nirvana but rather a path that leads to nirvana.

The Buddha also outlined a doctrine of moral action known as The Five Precepts (see the box on page 27). These precepts, along with other acts of compassion and justice, are necessary for progress along the Eightfold Path.

Much like all major religions are divided into different branches and denominations, Buddhism is divided into different schools; the most prominent are Theravada Buddhism and Mahayana Buddhism. The Theravada school is the smaller and more traditional of the two; Theravada Buddhists live mostly in Sri Lanka, southern India, Cambodia, Myanmar (Burma), and Thailand. Mahayana Buddhism is common in Tibet, Korea, Japan, and Nepal and is more open to new ideas and influences, allowing it to divide into a number of smaller schools, including Zen Buddhism. The chart below summarizes some of the major differences between the two traditions.

The Five Precepts

- Do not kill.
- Do not steal.
- Refrain from sexual misconduct.
- Do not lie.
- Refrain from intoxication.

Theravada	Mahayana
Nirvana: reached by one's individual efforts and practices	Nirvana: reached by the help of enlightened guides known as bodhisattvas
Key virtue: wisdom	Key virtue: compassion
Ritual and practice: a full-time job to be undertaken by monks and nuns in monasteries	Ritual and practice: incorporated into everyday life and undertaken by all adherents
Ideal: the enlightened individual who enters nirvana after death	Ideal: the enlightened bodhisattva who renounces nirvana to guide others
Texts: the teachings of the Buddha in the Pali Canon	Texts: the Sutras, which remain open and include commentaries and parables
Prayer: offered only through meditation to deepen faith and insight	Prayer: involves calling on Buddha for intervention and to answer petitions

Buddhist Sacred Texts

The Pali Canon is the preeminent scripture for Theravada Buddhists. Named for the language in which it was written, the Pali Canon was compiled in the first century B.C. and contains the Buddha's teachings and traditions that were passed down orally.

The most prominent Mahayana sacred text is the Lotus Sutra. Written in the first century A.D., the Lotus Sutra includes parables and accounts of the Buddha and portrays him as a divine and cosmic being. The Lotus Sutra also places a great deal of emphasis on *bodhisattvas*, enlightened persons who use their wisdom to help others find nirvana.

Buddhist Rituals

Buddhists seek to accumulate merit and good karma. One means of accumulating merit is *dana*, or donations. Monks and nuns make morning rounds carrying alms bowls to collect donations of food and money. These donations provide for the monks and nuns' daily needs; fund the monastery's work in education, health care, community service, and worship; and accumulate merit for the donor.

Chanting is a common ritual throughout Buddhism. Reciting chains of words (called *mantras*) from the sacred texts is believed to provide spiritual powers and create good karma. Thus chanting often accompanies meditation, worship, and rites of passage (such as birth, coming of age, marriage, and death). Chanting the Buddha's words while pouring water into a bowl is said to instill healing properties into the water. Those in need of purification can drink the transformed water or have it sprinkled over them.

Buddhists also visit shrines (sacred sites linked to the life and preaching of the Buddha) to access the shrine's healing powers and to earn merit. During their visits, visitors to shrines often practice other rituals such as meditation, chanting, and giving donations. Some devoted Buddhists even request that their cremated ashes be deposited on shrines.

In this Session

Youth should come away from this session with a very basic understanding of Buddhist history, beliefs, sacred texts, and practices. In particular youth should learn the following key points:

- The Buddha was a man named Siddhartha Gautama who was born in India in 563 B.C. He renounced his worldly possessions and escaped into the forest in search of enlightenment.

- *Buddha* literally means one who is "enlightened" to the reality that life is suffering (*dukkha*) and to the way to overcome suffering.

- *Samsâra*, much the same as in Hinduism, is a cycle of birth, life, death, and rebirth. The aim of Buddhism is *nirvana*, or libertation from samsâra.

- The Buddha taught the Four Noble Truths: 1) All life is suffering; 2) The cause of suffering is desire; 3) Overcoming desire removes suffering; and 4) Desire is overcome by following the Eightfold Path. (The Four Noble Truths and Eightfold Path are on pages 10–11 of the student book.)

- The two largest schools (denominations) of Buddhism are Theravada and Mahayana. The Pali Canon is the most sacred text for Theravada Buddhists; the most prominent scripture for Mahayana Buddhists is the Lotus Sutra.

Emphasize that Buddhism is an ancient, diverse, and complex faith and that this session covers only some of the basics.

Notes:

Getting Ready

As you prepare for this session, read the information about Buddhism on pages 24–29. If you have questions, additional resources are listed on pages 79–80 and at *burst.abingdonyouth.com.*

Keep in mind that Buddhism, like all of the faith traditions explored in this study, is an ancient and diverse faith practiced by millions of people. This program will cover only the basic beliefs and practices that are true for most Buddhists. Encourage your youth to refrain from drawing conclusions or making assumptions based on limited information. If they would like to learn more, point them to the additional resources on pages 79–80 and at *burst.abingdonyouth.com.* Also encourage them to talk to a practicing Buddhist.

If possible invite a Buddhist person from your community to talk to your youth about Buddhist beliefs and practices and to answer any questions the youth may have. (See "Dialogue With an Expert" on page 33.)

Food Ideas

Serve an assortment of vegetarian snacks. While Buddhists aren't required to be vegetarians, many choose to be vegetarians in order to minimize harm to other living beings.

Music Ideas

Play recordings of Buddhist chants. Several recordings of throat singing by Tibetan monks (such as The Gyuto Monks) are available at iTunes or other music stores.

Getting Ready: Read the article on pages 24–29 to help you answer basic questions about Buddhism. Also review the following activities and gather or prepare needed supplies.

ACTIVITIES	SUPPLIES
 Whaddaya Know (or Think You Know)? (10 minutes)	Sticky notes, pens or pencils
 The Truth Is Out There (5–10 minutes) **Preparation:** Write statements on markerboard (pages 32–33).	Markerboard, markers

Don't Forget to ...

 Dialogue With an Expert (15–20 minutes) **Preparation:** Invite a guest expert on Buddhism.	
 Four + Eight = Nirvana (10 minutes) **Preparation:** Review Four Noble Truths and Eightfold Path (page 26).	Information about Four Noble Truths and Eightfold Path (see student book (pages 10–11 or *burst.abingdonyouth.com*
 Assume the Lotus Position (15 minutes) **Preparation:** Inform parents (see page 34). Practice lotus positions ahead of time.	Small cushions, candles and matches
 Word Up (10–15 minutes) **Preparation:** Print copies of the Word Up: Buddhism worksheet.	Word Up: Buddhism worksheet, pens or pencils
 Sending Forth (5–10 minutes)	Candle, matches or lighter

Whaddaya Know (or Think You Know)?

To begin, set out several sticky notes and pens. Invite the youth to write on the sticky notes any information they know (or think they know) about Buddhism. They may also write any questions they have about Buddhism. Ask them to stick their notes on a markerboard or designated wall space.

> **You will need:** sticky notes and pens or pencils; if you have invited a guest expert, he or she could help with this activity.

When everyone has had an opportunity to contribute information and questions, ask the youth to organize the sticky notes. First, ask them to set aside the questions. Then ask them to work together to arrange the remaining stickies into three categories: 1) pretty sure it's true; 2) think it might be true; and 3) not sure if it's true.

If you have invited a Buddhist person to speak to your group (see Dialogue With an Expert on page 33), ask him or her to review the sticky notes and indicate which statements are true, which are true for some Buddhists but not others, which are partially true, and which are completely false.

If you do not have a visiting expert, verify as many of the facts and answer as many questions as possible using the information on pages 24–29 (see also below, "The Truth Is Out There").

Remind the youth that Buddhism, like Christianity and Hinduism, is a very diverse faith; that what is true for one Buddhist might not be true for all Buddhists; and that this session will focus on the beliefs and practices that most Buddhists have in common.

The Truth Is Out There

List on a markerboard the following common statements about Buddhism, some of which are true and some of which are false:

> **You will need:** a markerboard and markers.

  1. **All Buddhists are atheists.**

  2. **In Buddhism the goal of life is to overcome suffering and attain nirvana, or enlightenment.**

3. Siddhartha Gautama, the Buddha, was a Chinese prince.

4. For Buddhists, killing another living being results in bad karma.

5. The Buddha was a jolly, bald man with a fat, round belly.

6. For Buddhist monks, lunch is the final meal of the day.

For each statement, ask the youth to vote "true" or "false." The answers are: 1. *False—some Buddhists believe in a higher power, but this belief is not necessary for attaining nirvana*; 2. *True*; 3. *False— Siddhartha Gautama was an Indian prince*; 4. *False—killing another being brings bad karma only if it is intentional*; 5. *False—the chubby, laughing Buddha is actually Hotei, or Budai, a ninth-century Chinese monk*; 6. *True*.

Dialogue With an Expert

If possible, invite a Buddhist person from your community to explain to your youth the basics of his or her faith and to answer any questions they may have (such as those the youth wrote on the sticky notes).

> **You will need:** a guest expert on Buddhism.

Visit *burst.abingdonyouth.com* for a list of Buddhist temples in the United States. If there is not a temple in your community, check the faculty of a nearby university for an expert on Buddhism. If your guest requests a list of topics to cover, give him or her a list of the key points on page 29.

Four + Eight = Nirvana

Divide the youth into small groups, if possible separating the older (high school) youth from the younger (middle school youth). Assign an adult leader to each small group.

> **You will need:** student books or information from the website about the Four Noble Truths and Eightfold Path.

Instruct the groups to look at the Four Noble Truths on page 10 of the student book. (This information is also available at *burst.abingdonyouth.com*.) Give the groups a few minutes to discuss the following questions:

• Would you agree that all life is suffering? Why, or why not?

• Would you agree that desire causes suffering? Why, or why not?

• In what ways do Christians deal with desire and suffering?

Point out that the fourth Noble Truth states that the way to overcome desire is by following the Eightfold Path. Then instruct the groups to read about the Eightfold Path on page 11 of the student book. (This information is also available at *burst.abingdonyouth.com*.) Give the groups a few minutes to discuss the following questions:

• How might these eight steps help a person overcome desire and suffering?

• Why, do you think, is it important to have an occupation that is not harmful (to others and to the world)? What sorts of occupations might be considered harmful?

• Which of these steps are similar to Christian teachings? How?

Assume the Lotus Position

Note: Inform parents beforehand that youth will have an opportunity to practice Buddhist meditation. Explain that, during this exercise, youth will focus on their breathing and clear their minds. They will not be asked to pray to another god or perform any task that conflicts with Christian teaching. Respect the wishes of any parents or youth who are uncomfortable with this activity and would prefer not to participate.

You will need: if possible, one small cushion or pillow for each person; candles and matches.

Right concentration, or practicing advanced meditation, is the final step on the Eightfold Path. Provide youth an opportunity to experience Buddhist meditation (if only for a few minutes). Dim the lights and light several candles. Invite the youth to spread out in the meeting space and sit on the floor. If possible provide small pillows or cushions for sitting. Then ask them to assume the Lotus Position using the following instructions:

Half Lotus

1. In a sitting position, stretch your legs straight out in front of you.

2. Bend your left leg at the knee and bring it toward you so that you can take hold of your left foot with both hands.

3. Place your left foot so that the sole rests against the inside of your right thigh. The heel of your left foot should be drawn in as far as possible.

4. Bend your right leg at the knee so that you can take hold of your right foot with both hands.

5. Place your right foot in the fold of your left leg. Drop the right knee as far as possible toward the floor. Rest your hands on your knees.

6. When your legs grow tired, stretch them straight out in front of you and gently massage your knees. Then reverse your legs so that the right leg is drawn in first and the left leg is on top.

Full Lotus

The Full Lotus is similar to the Half Lotus, but both feet should be placed on top of the opposite thigh and the knees should rest on the ground. This position requires advanced flexibility and may not be possible for most youth.

Ask the youth to sit with a straight back and neck (no slouching). Their arms should be outstretched with the backs of their hands resting on their knees. Their hands should be in a relaxed position with the thumb and forefinger slightly touching.

Instruct students to close their eyes, remain silent, and focus simply on breathing in and out their noses at a slow, controlled pace. Do this for five minutes.

Ask the youth to react to the experience: What did they like about this practice? What made them uncomfortable? Were they able to clear their minds and rest? You might comment that many Christians also practice silent meditation as a way to clear their minds and focus on God or ask the youth how this exercise is like or unlike silent prayer.

Word Up

Hand out copies of the Word Up: Buddhism worksheet. Explain that youth will match terms and concepts associated with Buddhism. This handout is available at *burst.abingdonyouth.com*. Challenge youth, working individually or in teams, to match the terms to their correct definitions. The answers are:

You will need: copies of the Word Up: Buddhism worksheet, pens or pencils.

bodhisattva (boh-dee-SAHT-vah): an enlightened person who renounces nirvana to help others achieve salvation

buddha: an enlightened person, or one who has awakened to the truth

The Buddha: Siddhartha Gautama, who sat beneath a ficus tree until he had rid himself of ego and desire and achieved enlightenment

Dalai Lama: the spiritual leader of Tibetan Buddhists

dharma: the teachings of the Buddha

dukkha: the Pali language word meaning suffering

the lotus position: the posture that Buddhists take during meditation

mantra: a verse of syllables, believed to be of divine origin, used in meditation or other rituals

Mahayana: a type of Buddhism common in Tibet, Japan, and Korea. Of the two main schools of Buddhism, it is the one most open to new ideas and influences.

nirvana: the final goal of Buddhism—the complete elimination of suffering

Pali Canon: the main sacred text for Theravada Buddhists

sutras: collections of the Buddha's teachings

Theravada: a traditional or conservative type of Buddhism that is common in Sri Lanka, southern India, and southeast Asia

Thich Nhat Hahn (TIK NYAT HAN): a well-known Vietnamese Buddhist monk, teacher, poet, author, and activist

Zen: a form of Mahayana Buddhism that is popular in the west and emphasizes meditation and mindfulness of one's experiences

As time permits, you may elaborate on some of these definitions and descriptions using the information on pages 24–28.

Sending Forth

Gather the youth in a circle, dim the lights, and light a candle. Say: "Today we learned some of the basics of Buddhism. Buddhism has Four Noble Truths. To close, I want you to think about the key truths of Christianity." (Since overcoming desire and eliminating suffering are major emphases in Buddhism, you might also ask the youth to reflect on how Christians deal with desire and suffering and what Christians might learn from Buddhists about this subject.)

> **You will need:** a candle and matches.

Pass around the candle. Invite each person, when holding the candle, to name something he or she learned about Buddhism and one major truth of Christianity. Then close in prayer, thanking God for the opportunity to gather as a Christian community to learn about Buddhism.

JUDAISM

Thou shalt love thy neighbour as thyself.
—Leviticus 19:18b

That which is despicable to you, do not do to
your fellow, this is the whole Torah, and the rest
is commentary, go and learn it.
—Talmud, Shabbat 31a

Introduction

The Story of Judaism

It is difficult to give a date for the birth of Judaism. Some trace its religious origins back to Noah and the flood, others to Moses on Sinai, the rebuilding of the Temple in Jerusalem following the Exile in Babylon, or the destruction of the second Temple in A.D. 70. We'll begin our look at Judaism with the story of Abraham.

Genesis tells the story of Abram, a son of Terah in the lineage of Noah's son Shem. (The word *Semite* is derived from "Shem.") God called Abram, his wife Sarai, and their family to settle in the land of Canaan, where their descendents would become a great nation. God made a covenant with Abram and Sarai and changed their names to Abraham and Sarah. Eventually Sarah, despite being well past childbearing age, gave birth to a son: Isaac. Isaac's son Jacob, whom God renamed Israel, fathered twelve sons, each of whom became the father of one of the twelve tribes of Israel.

During a great famine, the people of Israel migrated to Egypt (see **Genesis 37, 39–50**.) The Israelites increased in number, and the Egyptian pharaoh considered them to be a threat and forced them into slavery. But in slavery the Israelites became even more numerous until Pharaoh ordered all newborn Israelite boys to be killed. One very special child escaped: Moses. God called Moses to lead Israel out of slavery and back to Canaan, the Promised Land.

After forty years of traveling through the desert, the Israelites returned to Canaan and, under the leadership of Moses' successor Joshua, settled the land as a confederation of twelve tribes. Eventually pressure from neighboring lands forced the twelve tribes to unite as a monarchy. The prophet Samuel anointed Saul as the first king of Israel. David succeeded Saul and made Jerusalem the holy capital of the Kingdom of Israel. Solomon inherited the kingdom from his father and oversaw the building of the Temple in Jerusalem. After Solomon's death, a power struggle resulted in Israel's split into two kingdoms: Israel in the north and Judah in the south. "Jew" and "Judaism" are derived from "Judah."

In the eighth century B.C., the Assyrians conquered the Northern Kingdom of Israel and took captive many of its people. In 587 B.C. Judah also fell, this time to the Babylonian Empire. The Babylonians destroyed Jerusalem and the Temple and forced many of Judah's people into exile. After Persia conquered Babylon in 539, the Persian king Cyrus allowed the exiles to return and rebuild the Temple. The former Kingdom of Judah became the province of Judea. Many of the exiled Jewish people did not return, forming Jewish communities outside Judea. The next several centuries witnessed the settlement of important Jewish communities in Babylon, Africa, Greece, and Asia Minor (current-day Turkey). While Jerusalem remained the center of Jewish identity, "Judaism was well on the way to redefining itself as a religion that could be carried anywhere in the world."[1]

By the time of Jesus, several movements had developed within Judaism. The Pharisees, one prominent and influential group, were experts in the *Torah*, or law. (Many Christians only know the Pharisees as religious teachers who opposed Jesus. These Pharisees are not representative of the group as a whole.) They were well-versed both in the written Torah (Genesis, Exodus, Leviticus, Numbers, and Deuteronomy) and in the oral Torah (the oral traditions that had been passed down along with the written Torah). After the Romans destroyed the second Temple in Jerusalem in A.D. 70, many Jews questioned how their tradition would survive apart from the Temple and the rituals performed there. The Pharisees were able to draw from the oral tradition to interpret the requirements of Jewish life in light of these new circumstances. They interpreted the Temple rituals as acts of holiness and taught that holiness could be expressed

Judaism   **39**

through studying the Torah, worshiping in the synagogue, and acts of loving kindness. The oral traditions eventually were recorded in the Talmud (more below). Those who taught and interpreted the Torah and Talmud became known as *rabbis*, meaning "teachers."

The history of the Jewish people is rife with examples of oppression and exile. But neither the Jewish people nor their ancestors had experienced the level and breadth of persecution that came in the form of The Final Solution of the Jewish Question in Europe, Nazi Germany's platform of complete Jewish annihilation that began with Hitler's rise to power in 1933. By first limiting the rights of Jewish persons and then relegating them to ghettos, quarantining them in concentration camps, and finally murdering them en masse, Hitler and the Nazi party attempted to wipe out all the Jews in Europe. By 1945 six million Jewish persons had been killed, constituting forty percent of the world's Jewish population.

From the ashes of the most devastating event in Jewish history (and modern human history) rose one of the greatest. On May 14, 1948, the sovereign Jewish nation of Israel declared independence. But on May 15 an allied army of seven nearby Arab states invaded Israel, refusing to recognize its sovreignty. War and conflict between Israel and its neighbors have continued throughout the past sixty years.

Jewish Essentials

At the heart of Judaism is **Deuteronomy 6:4-9**, known as the *Shema*. (*Shema* is the Hebrew word for "hear.") The Shema begins, "Hear O Israel: The LORD is our God, the LORD alone. You shall love the LORD your God with all your heart, and with all your soul, and with all your might" (verses 4–5). Loving God in this way means doing what God commands. "Judaism is a religion of responsibility: It is not what we believe, it is what we do and how we act," says Rabbi Saul Strosberg. He goes on to say, "When we go to heaven, we believe God is not going to say, 'What did you believe?' God is going to say, 'What did you do?'" So what does God want us to do?

Perhaps the best way to describe Judaism is as a religion wholly devoted to God and to doing good deeds for others. Actions such as feeding the hungry or caring for the sick or giving to the poor are not merely options for Jews—they are commandments, or *mitzvot,* and keeping these commandments is a way to keeping the covenants that God established with them through Abraham and Sarah and Moses and David. These covenants are why Jews are called God's "chosen people." The Jewish people are not chosen because they are endowed with special gifts, traits, or privileges, but because they are chosen by God to keep the commandments.

While these essentials are common throughout Judaism, the Jewish faith (like the other faiths included in this study) is very diverse. In the United States today there are four main branches or denominations of Judaism: Orthodox, Conservative, Reform, and Reconstructionist. A chart detailing the differences between these denominations can be found at *burst.abingdonyouth.com*.

Jewish Sacred Texts

The Torah is Judaism's most sacred text. *Torah* literally means "law" and refers to the five books of Moses: Genesis, Exodus, Leviticus, Numbers, and Deuteronomy. The Torah is also the first of three sections of the *Tanak*, or Jewish Bible. The second is the *Nevi'im*, or prophets: Joshua, Judges, Samuel, Kings, Isaiah, Jeremiah, Ezekiel, and the Twelve Prophets (Hosea–Malachi in Christian Bibles). The third part is the *Ketuvim*, or writings: Psalms, Proverbs, Job, Song of Songs, Ruth, Lamentations, Ecclesiastes, Esther, Daniel, Ezra and Nehemiah, and Chronicles. The initials of these three sections, TNK, with vowels added, create the name *Tanak*.

In a larger sense *Torah* refers to the entirety of Jewish law and teaching, both the written Torah and the oral Torah, or *Talmud*. The Talmud consists of the *Mishnah*, a written collection organized by subject of oral traditions and commentaries, and the *Gemara*, a written account of rabbinic discussions about the Mishnah. These commentaries help present-day believers interpret ancient rules in light of modern sensitivities.

Jewish Holidays and Rituals

A key component of Judaism is the observance of holidays, festivals, and life-cycle events. Rabbi Irving Greenberg claims that

Jewish Holidays

Shabbat: the sabbath day, from sundown on Friday until sundown on Saturday

Pesach: Passover, the eight-day festival celebrating Israel's liberation from slavery in Egypt

Shavuot: The Festival of Weeks commemorating the first fruits of the spring harvest and Moses receiving the Torah on Mt. Sinai

Rosh Hashanah: the New Year and a time of solemn reflection on the past year

Yom Kippur: the Day of Atonement, when Jews repent of their sins and spend the day in prayer and fasting

Sukkot: the Feast of Booths, an eight-day festival marking the autumn harvest

Chanukah: an eight-day commemoration of the rededication of the Jerusalem Temple after it was profaned by Antiochus IV in 165 B.C.E.

Brit Milah: the ritual of circumcision that takes place eight days after birth

Bar Mitzvah/Bat Mitzvah: meaning "[son or daughter] of the commandments," when a young person turns 13 (boys) or 12 (girls), he or she inherits responsibilities for maintaining the Jewish community

the recurrence of holidays marks the very experiences of Jewish life. (See the list in the box to the left.) More detailed information is available at *burst.abingdon youth.com.*

Keeping *kosher*, or following dietary restrictions from the Torah, is a part of day-to-day Jewish life. According to Rabbi Morris Kertzer, every Jew decides the extent to which he or she keeps kosher. Some of the important rules are:

• One may eat only the meat of animals that chew their cud and have cloven hooves; thus, pork is rejected.

• One may eat only fish with fins and scales. Shellfish are restricted.

• One may not eat birds that prey on other animals.

• Animals must be slaughtered by trained individuals in a specific way that does not cause unnecessary pain.

• Meat products and dairy products may not be cooked or eaten together.

[1] Raymond Scheindlin, *A Short History of the Jewish People* (Oxford: Oxford Press, 1998); page 49.

Burst: World Religions

In this Session

Youth should come away from this session with a very basic understanding of Jewish beliefs, sacred texts, and practices. In particular, youth should learn the following key points:

- Judaism, like Christianity and Islam (which you'll explore in the next session), traces its roots back to **Abraham**.

- The **Torah** is Judaism's most sacred text. *Torah* literally means "law" and refers to the five books of Moses: Genesis, Exodus, Leviticus, Numbers, and Deuteronomy. The Torah is also the first of three sections of the *Tanak*, or Jewish Bible.

- In a larger sense *Torah* refers to the entirety of Jewish law and teaching, both the written Torah and the oral Torah, or *Talmud*. The Talmud is a collection of oral teachings that help Jews interpret and apply the Torah.

- The **Tanak**, or Jewish Bible, is not the same as the Christian Old Testament. While the books are the same, there are significant differences in the order, translation, and interpretation of these books.

- Observing and keeping the Jewish **rituals, traditions, and holidays** is an important way in which Jewish people connect to God, their history, and Jewish people around the world. These traditions include keeping **kosher**, observing **Shabbat** (the sabbath), and celebrating **bat and bar mitzvahs**.

Be clear that Judaism is an ancient, diverse, and complex faith and that this session can cover only some of the basics.

Getting Ready

As you prepare for this session, read the material about Judaism on pages 38–43. If you have questions, additional resources are listed on on pages 79–80 and at *burst.abingdonyouth.com.*

Keep in mind that Judaism, like all of the faith traditions explored in this study, is an ancient and diverse faith practiced by millions of people. This program will cover only the basic beliefs and practices that are true for most Jewish persons. Encourage your youth to refrain from drawing conclusions or making assumptions based on limited information. (This is especially important with regards to Judaism. Since Christians share a common heritage with Jews, we often think we know more about Judaism than we actually do.) If youth would like to learn more, point them to the additional resources on pages 79–80 and at *burst.abingdonyouth.com.* Also encourage them to talk to an observant Jew.

If possible invite a Jewish person from your community to talk to your youth about Jewish beliefs and practices and to answer any questions the youth may have. (See "Dialogue With an Expert" on page 49.)

✾ Food Ideas

Consider serving a kosher meal. (See "Sabbath Supper" on pages 46–47.) You might also check out some of the kosher snack foods available at Thou Shall Snack (*www.thoushallsnack.com*).

✾ Music Ideas

Jewish music in a variety of styles and from a variety of traditions is available from online music stores such as Jewish Music (*www.jewishmusic.com*) and jtunes (*www.jtunes.com*).

Getting Ready: Read the article on pages 38–43 to help you answer basic questions about Judaism. Also review the following activities and gather or prepare needed supplies.

<u>ACTIVITIES</u>	<u>SUPPLIES</u>
🍥 **Sabbath Supper (20 minutes)** **Preparation:** Read pages 46–47.	**Prepared sabbath foods**
🍥 **Whaddaya Know (or Think You Know)? (10 minutes)**	
🍥 **The Truth Is Out There (5–10 minutes)** **Preparation:** Write statements on page 48 on a markerboard.	**Markerboard, markers**
🍥 **Dialogue With an Expert (15–20 minutes)** **Preparation:** Invite a guest expert on Judaism.	
🍥 **Mitzvot and Mishnah (10 minutes)** **Preparation:** Review information on pages 48–49.	**Bibles**
🍥 **Word Up (10–15 minutes)** **Preparation:** Copy and cut apart the Word Up: Judaism cards.	**Word Up: Judaism cards, pens or pencils, scissors**
🍥 **Sending Forth (5–10 minutes)**	**Candle, matches or lighter**

Don't Forget to . . .

Shabbat Practice

The *Shabbat*, or sabbath, is an important time of rest and reflection for Jewish people. There are thirty-nine categories of activities from which religiously observant Jews abstain during Shabbat; these categories mainly involve the creation of food, shelter, and clothing. (Interpretations of these restrictions vary.) Shabbat allows Jewish people to spend time with God, friends, and family without being hindered by work or obligation.

During your time together, try "keeping sabbath" by adhering to the following rules. Some of these will require you to plan and prepare ahead of time, much as Jewish families must prepare for Shabbat.

- Wear nice clothes (what we Christians might call our "Sunday best").

- If you plan to serve a meal or snack during your meeting time, prepare it ahead of time so that everyone can rest from preparing meals; serve only kosher foods. (See the information on page 42.)

- Instruct the youth to leave all electronic devices at home (or turn them off and put them away) so that they can rest from worldly attachments.

- Do not light a fire, or do not turn on the lights. Remember to light candles (or turn lights on earlier) so that you can rest from your dependence on resources other than God.

- Do not write or erase anything.

Sabbath Supper

Consider eating a kosher meal together as a group. Prepare all of the dishes beforehand so that you don't do any work during your sabbath time. (See "Shabbat Practice" above.) Include the following foods:

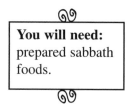

You will need: prepared sabbath foods.

- **Challah** (KHAH-luh) is a traditional braided loaf of bread that is often served at Shabbat meals and can be purchased at many bakeries.

Burst: World Religions

- **Cholent** (CHAW-luhnt) is a traditional Shabbat dish of meat and beans that can be cooked slowly on a stove or in a slow cooker before the beginning of Shabbat. (A recipe for cholent is available at *burst.abingdonyouth.com*.)

(You may need to provide a kosher vegetarian alternative for youth who don't eat meat.)

As you eat together, explain to the youth that challah and cholent are traditional foods eaten by Jewish people on Shabbat, or the sabbath. Talk about Shabbat using the information on page 46 and from the Jewish Holidays handout (available at *burst.abingdonyouth.com*). Also explain that these foods are kosher and were prepared in accordance with the dietary laws in the Torah (what we know as the first five books of the Old Testament) and talk about some of the kosher regulations listed on page 42.

Whaddaya Know (or Think You Know)?

Divide the youth into groups of four or five and invite them to talk about what they know or think they know about Judaism and to voice any questions they have about Judaism. (If possible, assign an adult to each small group.) In their groups ask youth to identify facts about Judaism that they think are true. After several minutes, invite each group to report on its facts and questions about Judaism.

> **You will need:** no supplies; if you have invited a guest expert, he or she could help with this activity.

If you have invited a Jewish expert to speak to your group (see "Dialogue With an Expert" on page 49), ask him or her to confirm the facts or (gently) explain why they are false or only partially true.

If you do not have an expert, verify as many of the facts and answer as many questions as possible using the information on pages 38–43. Some of these facts and questions might also be covered in "The Truth Is Out There" (see page 48).

Remind the youth that Judaism, like Christianity, Hinduism, and Buddhism, is a very diverse faith; that what is true for one Jewish person may not be true for all Jewish persons; and that this session will focus on the beliefs and practices that most Jewish people have in common.

The Truth Is Out There

Beforehand list on a markerboard the following common statements about Judaism, some of which are true and some of which are false:

> **You will need:** a markerboard and markers.

1. **In the Jewish tradition, a day runs from one sundown to the next sundown.**

2. **It is impossible to convert to Judaism.**

3. **Observant Jews do not eat pork.**

4. **Jesus renounced his Jewish faith.**

5. **Chanukah (or Hannukah) is the most important Jewish holiday.**

6. **The Jewish Bible is the same as the Christian Old Testament.**

7. **Jews are still waiting for the coming messiah.**

8. **During the Holocaust, the Nazis targeted both religious and non-religious Jews.**

For each statement ask the youth to vote "true" or "false." The answers are: 1. *True—on the Jewish calendar, the day is modeled on* **Genesis 1:5** *("And there was evening and there was morning, the first day")*; 2. *False—while Judaism does not seek converts, all major Jewish denominations accept converts*; 3. *True—see the information about keeping kosher on page 42*; 4. *False—Jesus lived and taught as a Jew and followed Jewish customs*; 5. *False—Chanukah actually is one of the least important Jewish holidays*; 6. *False—while all the books of our Old Testament are found in the Jewish Bible, or* Tanak, *the translation and the order and combination of books (Ezra and Nehemiah are one book, for example) are different*; 7. *True <u>and</u> false—some Jews, such as Orthodox Jews, pray for the coming of a* *messiah, while others, such as Reform Jews, look forward to a messianic age of peace and justice but do not believe in an individual messiah; 8. True—Jews were targeted for their ethnicity and culture as well as their religious beliefs.*

Dialogue With an Expert

If possible invite a rabbi or other leader from a nearby synagogue or temple to explain to your youth the basics of Judaism and to answer any questions they have (such as those they talked about earlier). If your guest

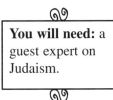

You will need: a guest expert on Judaism.

requests a list of topics to cover, provide the key points on page 43.

Mitzvot and Mishnah

Ask the youth if they have ever attended a friend's bat mitzvah or bar mitzvah. Allow youth who have attended these ceremonies to talk about what they saw and experienced.

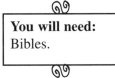

You will need: Bibles.

Explain that *bar* or *bat mitzvah* literally means "son or daughter of the commandment." When a Jewish boy or girl celebrates his or her bar or bat mitzvah, he or she is recognized as an adult and is responsible for keeping the commandments and maintaining the Jewish community. (If time permits, you might ask youth to talk about how bat and bar mitzvahs are similar to confirmation in Christian churches.)

Hand out Bibles and divide the youth into pairs or small groups. Say: "Most of you are familiar with the Ten Commandments, but there are a lot more than ten commandments, or mitzvot, in the Torah— Genesis, Exodus, Leviticus, Numbers, and Deuteronomy." (*Mitzvot* is the plural of *mitzvah*.) Challenge the pairs or teams to look through the first five books of the Bible and guess the total number of commandments. They won't have time to count them all. Give them a few minutes to formulate their guesses, then reveal that Jewish tradition recognizes 613 mitzvot in the Torah.

Say: "*Torah*, meaning 'law,' is the first of three sections of the Jewish Bible, or *Tanak*. The Tanak contains the same writings as our Old

Testament, but they're organized differently and there are some differences in translation and interpretation." Point out the information about the Jewish scriptures on page 13 of the student book. Explain that the *Talmud*, a written compilation of oral teachings, also is important in Judaism. The Talmud includes the *Mishnah*, teachings that interpret the Torah and apply it to people's lives, and the *Gemara*, a written account of discussions among rabbis about the Mishnah.

Word Up

Beforehand copy and cut apart the Word Up: Judaism cards so that you can provide a set of cards for every three or four youth. These are available at *burst.abingdonyouth.com*. Challenge youth, working in teams of three or four, to match the terms to their correct definitions. The answers are:

> **You will need:** copies of the Word Up: Judaism cards.

> **bar mitzvah/bat mitzvah:** literally means "[son or daughter] of the commandment." When Jewish youth turn 13 (boys) or 12 (girls), these ceremonies recognize them as adults who are responsible for keeping the commandments.

> **Diaspora:** Jewish communities outside of the land of Israel

> **halakhah:** a particular way of life that involves adherence to the Jewish law

> **Israel:** 1. the name God gave to Jacob; 2. the nation formed by Jacob's descendents; 3. the kingdom ruled by Saul, David, and Solomon; 4. the "Northern Kingdom" after Solomon's death; 5. a nation in the Middle East founded in 1948

> **mitzvot:** commandments; also can refer to good deeds

> **Pesach:** the Passover; the eight-day festival celebrating Israel's liberation from slavery in Egypt

> **rabbi:** literally means "teacher"; an interpreter of the Torah and a spiritual leader in current-day Jewish communities

> **Rosh Hashanah:** the Jewish New Year

Shabbat: the sabbath, from sundown Friday until sundown Saturday

synagogue: where Jews gather for worship and study

Talmud: a written compilation of oral traditions, commentaries, and rabbinic teaching; consists of the Mishnah and the Gemara

Tanak: the Jewish Bible; consists of the Torah, Nevi'im, and Ketuvim

Torah: 1. the first five books of the Tanak; 2. the entire collection of Jewish sacred texts; 3. the Jewish way of life

Yom Kippur: the Day of Atonement, when Jewish persons repent of their sins and spend the day in prayer and fasting

Sending Forth

Gather the youth in a circle. Go around the circle and ask each youth to name one fact about Judaism that he or she didn't know prior to this session. Then move around the circle a second time asking each person to name something about Christianity that people outside the church might not know. Say: "There are many things that people of different faith traditions don't know or understand about one another. We need to be careful not to make assumptions about what people of other faiths believe. We also need to be able to articulate to others what we, as Christians, believe and do."

Close with the following prayer, the Kiddush, which is traditionally prayed at the sabbath dinner:

> Let us praise God with this symbol of joy, and give God thanks for the blessings of the past week: for life and strength, for home and love and friendship, for the discipline of our trials and temptations, for the happiness that has come to us out of our labors. You have ennobled us, O God, with the blessings of work, and in love You have sanctified us by Sabbath rest and worship.[2]

[2] Morris Kertzer, *What Is a Jew?* (New York: Touchstone, 1998); pages 212–213.

ISLAM

None of you [truly] believes until he wishes for his brother what he wishes for himself.
—Number 13 of Imam Al-Nawawi's Forty Hadiths

Introduction

Islam arguably is the most misunderstood and misrepresented religion included in this study. Many in the western world associate Islam with religious extremism, terrorism, and war. This image is far removed from the essential beliefs and practices of Islam (which comes from the Arabic word meaning "peace" and "surrender"). This session will explore some of these beliefs and practices along with Islam's history and sacred writings.

The Story of Islam

Like Jews and Christians, Muslims, those who follow Islam, trace their roots through Abraham back to the creation of the world and humanity. The three faiths all worship the God of Abraham—"Allah" simply is the Arabic word for God—and recognize many of the same ancient heroes and leaders. The Quran (Koran) says in 3:84:

> Say ye: "We believe in Allah and what has been revealed to us, and what was revealed to Abraham and Ishmael, and Isaac, and Jacob and his children, and what was given to Moses and Jesus, and what was given to all other Prophets from their Lord. We make no difference between any of them; and to Him we submit ourselves."

While Islam often is considered the newest major world religion, Muslims would argue that Islam is not a new religion at all but is part of a religious tradition that stretches as far back as creation. Genesis tells us that, because Abraham's wife Sarah was unable to conceive children, Abraham conceived a child, Ishmael, with Sarah's servant Hagar. But when God later blessed Sarah with a son, Isaac, Hagar and Ishmael were sent away. Muslims believe that Abraham went with Hagar and Ishmael to a place in Arabia, now called Mecca, and built with Ishmael a house of worship. It was from here that

Ishmael's descendants became a great and prosperous nation. (**Genesis 21** tells the story of God's promise to "make a great nation of [Ishmael]"; see verse 18b).

But by the middle of the sixth century A.D., the people of Arabia were living in chaos. Muslims use the word *ignorant* to describe this time. Against this backdrop in A.D. 570, Muhammad ibn Abdullah was born in the city of Mecca. His parents died when he was very young, so Muhammad was raised by his uncle and worked very hard to help support his family. When he was twenty-five, Muhammad married a woman named Khadija, and they started a family.

Muhammad became known in Mecca as a responsible and trustworthy businessman, but the moral depravity of the culture in which he lived burdened him deeply. He began retreating to a cave in nearby Mount Hira and praying to Allah, the God of the Jews and Christians, whom Arabs at the time considered one god of many. Muhammad prayed to Allah exclusively. Muslims believe that one night in 610 the angel Gabriel appeared to Muhammad in the cave and instructed him to read some verses from a piece of parchment. These verses instructed Muhammad to proclaim God's message as God's prophet. On this night Muhammad became the "Seal of the Prophets"—the last in a long line of prophets including Moses, Elijah, and Jesus.

Muhammad continued receiving revelations from God and spent the next several years in Mecca preaching God's message and living it out in his personal life. He preached that Allah was the one true God and rejected polytheism and idol worship; he preached against exploiting the poor; and he preached a message of justice and equality for those who were marginalized (including women). His message was aimed at the corrupt leaders in Mecca, and they did not like what they were hearing.

Muhammad and his small group of followers were ostracized and forced to flee Mecca. One night in 622, Muhammad and the Muslim faithful migrated to a nearby city now known as Medina. There his message flourished and began to spread throughout Arabia. So important was Muhammad's move from Mecca to Medina that the Muslim calendar begins not with the prophet's birth but with the date of his *hijra* (immigration to Medina).

Islam

By the time of his death in 632, Muhammad had practically unified Arabia and had established Islam as a major regional influence. This influence continued to grow after Muhammad's death. Over the next several centuries, Islam went from being a regional religion to being a truly global faith. Muhammad's successors, known as *caliphs*, gave rise to the *ulama*, an institution of religious scholars who advanced Muslim influence by establishing a law based on the example of the Prophet Muhammad (*sunna*) and on Islam's holy text, the Quran. Islamic law (*sharia*) addressed religious and political realities and came to serve as a blueprint for Muslim life and society. It covers practices of worship and devotion as well as regulations for public life, banking and inheritance, and marriage and divorce. The development of Islamic law laid the foundation for a Muslim empire that would stretch across South Asia, the Middle East, and parts of Europe.

In 1095 Pope Urban II called on Christians to unite in a Holy War against Muslims. For two centuries, battles known as the Crusades raged across the Middle East and central Europe, wiping out entire communities on both sides. The Crusades left many Muslims with a distrust and negative perception of Christianity and the western world.

Islamic culture continued to thrive even after the Crusades. For several centuries, the Ottoman Empire, a Muslim empire, controlled much of the Middle East, North Africa, and southeastern Europe. But by the nineteenth century, the empire had begun to loose strength, in part due to European colonial powers such as Britain and France which occupied Muslim lands. Muslims struggled to respond to modernity and the Christian colonizers. Some wanted to reinterpret Islamic law to fit the modern world, while others wanted modernity to conform to Islamic law. Some favored secularism and the separation of religion and government, while others wanted to reintroduce an Islamic state. These different approaches still persist today.

Muslim Beliefs

In the pre-dawn hours in Muslim communities worldwide, a voice can be heard crying out in Arabic the simple phrase, "There is no god but God." Muslims believe that this same phrase burst forth from the cave in Mount Hira when Muhammad received his call to be a prophet, and it remains an essential Muslim belief. Another key tenet of Islam is the unique roll to which God called Muhammad. These two beliefs form the Muslim affirmation of faith: "There is no god but God, and Muhammad is His Prophet." All other Muslim beliefs extend from this basic affirmation.

Muslims believe that God is transcendent and that we cannot comprehend God without an intermediary. The Prophet Muhammad and the Quran are the two intermediaries through which Muslims know God.

Muslim Sacred Texts

Muhammad saw himself as part of the Jewish and Christian tradition. And he believed that he was called not to start a new religion but to reform the old. Muslims believe that human editing and interpretation corrupted God's message in the Hebrew Scriptures and in the New Testament. Thus God chose to give Muhammad a final, pure revelation in the Quran. Muslims believe that God alone is the author of the Quran and that Muhammad was merely the vehicle through which God chose to communicate and disseminate it.

According to Muslim belief, God first revealed the Quran to Muhammad during the prophet's visits to Mount Hira. These revelations continued over the next twenty years. The final composition is believed to be eternal, unchangeable, perfect, and divine. The Quran contains 114 *suras* (chapters) and more than six thousand verses about God's existence, sovereignty, and will. Much the same as Christians believe that Jesus is the Word of God in human form, Muslims believe that the Quran is the Word of God in book form. For this reason the Quran is a holy relic and must not be defiled or destroyed.

Muslims also draw wisdom from *hadiths*, oral accounts of Muhammad's words and deeds that help Muslims better follow the prophet's example. There is no official written collection of hadiths, but Muslim scholars go to great lengths to determine which are authentic and worthy of emulating.

The Five Pillars of Islam

Shahada: the profession, "There is no god but God, and Muhammad is His Prophet." Muslims repeat this phrase multiple times each day.

Salat: prayer five times per day: dawn, noon, mid-afternoon, sunset, and night. In Muslim communities the voice of a *muezzin* (moo-EHZ-zin) calls people to prayer at the appointed times.

Zakat: the giving of alms or charity. The Quran stipulates that followers give 2.5 percent of all their income and assets for relief to the poor and needy.

Sawm: fast during Ramadan. During the sacred month of Ramadan, Muslims are required to fast from sunrise to sunset to practice self-discipline and acknowledge their dependence on God.

Hajj: pilgrimage to Mecca. Those who are physically able and who have the financial means are required to make at least one trip to the birthplace of Islam.

Muslim Practices and Rituals

Muslim belief is manifest in the Five Pillars of Islam (see descriptions of these five essential practices in the box).

In addition to the Five Pillars, several other practices are common across Islam. *Sawm*, one of the pillars, involves fasting during Ramadan, the sacred month in which Muhammad first received his call to be a prophet. Ramadan ends with a three-day celebration called *Id al-Fitr*—the Feast of the Breaking of the Fast. Another celebration, *Id al-Adha*, falls several months after Ramadan and commemorates Abraham and Ishmael's obedience to God when God commanded Abraham to sacrifice Ishmael. (Christians and Jews believe that God told Abraham to sacrifice Isaac, not Ishmael.) It is also a time to give thanks to God for staying Abraham's hand so that Ishmael could live and give birth to a great nation.

Like other religions, Islam celebrates key life-cycle events such as birth, marriage, and coming of age. When a young person reaches maturity, he or she participates in an initiation ceremony called "taking *shahada*" in which he or she repeats the profession of faith: "There is no god but God, and Muhammad is His Prophet."

In This Session

Youth should come away from this session with a very basic understanding of Islamic history, beliefs, sacred texts, and practices. In particular youth should learn the following key points:

- Islam, like Christianity and Judaism, traces its roots back to **Abraham**. Muslims consider Abraham's first son Ishmael the father of the Arab people.

- Muslims consider **Muhammad** the last and greatest of the prophets.

- Muslims believe that the **Quran**, which God revealed to Muhammad, is the eternal and perfect Word of God.

- The **Five Pillars of Islam** are practices required of all Muslims. They are: *shahada* (profession that "there is no god but God, and Muhammad is His Prophet); *salat* (prayer five times per day); *zakat* (almsgiving); *sawm* (fasting during the month of Ramadan); and *hajj* (pilgrimage to Mecca).

Emphasize that Islam is an ancient, diverse, and complex faith and that this session covers only some of the basics.

A Note on Sunni and Shia

The majority of the world's Muslims are Sunni Muslims. "Sunni" is derived from the word *sunna*, which refers to the example and teaching of Muhammad. Shia Islam is the largest minority sect and is the majority religion in Iran and Iraq. Shia Muslims believe that Muhammad appointed his son-in-law, Ali, as his successor and that Muslim leaders should come from Muhammad's family. There are several offshoots and branches of these two sects. Groups of mystics known as Sufis can be found in both sects.

Getting Ready

As you prepare for this session, read the material about Islam on pages 52–57. If you have questions about what you have read, additional resources are listed on pages 79–80 and at *burst.abingdon youth.com.*

Keep in mind that Islam, like all of the faith traditions in this study, is an ancient and diverse faith practiced by millions of people. This session explores only the basic beliefs and practices that are true for most Muslim persons. Encourage your youth to refrain from drawing conclusions or making assumptions based on limited information. If youth would like to learn more, point them to the additional resources on pages 79–80 and at *burst.abingdonyouth.com.* Also encourage them to talk to a Muslim.

If possible invite a Muslim person from your community to talk to your youth about Muslim beliefs and practices and to answer any questions the youth may have. (See "Dialogue With an Expert" on page 61.)

℅ Food Ideas

Consider serving Middle Eastern foods such as pita bread with hummus or a yogurt dip, falafel, and Baba ghanoush. Keep in mind that Muslims observe dietary restrictions that prohibit many types of meat.

℅ Music Ideas

Islam has a rich tradition of readers who recite passages from the Quran (always in Arabic) according to strict rules of pronunciation, intonation, and rhythm. These recitations have a melodic quality and will give you a sense of one way in which Muslims experience their sacred text. You can purchase these from online music stores such as iTunes.

Getting Ready: Read the article on pages 52–57 to help you answer basic questions about Islam. Also review the following activities and gather or prepare needed supplies.

ACTIVITIES	SUPPLIES
✿ **Whaddaya Know (or Think You Know)? (10 minutes)**	Sticky notes, pens or pencils
✿ **The Truth Is Out There (5–10 minutes)** **Preparation:** Write the statements on pages 60–61 on a markerboard.	Markerboard, markers
✿ **Dialogue With an Expert (15–20 minutes)** **Preparation:** Invite a guest expert on Islam.	
✿ **The Word of God (10 minutes)** **Preparation:** See *www.abingdon youth.com/burst* for recordings.	Bibles, Quran recitation recordings, a copy of the Quran is optional.
✿ **Five Pillars (10 minutes)** **Preparation:** Review the Five Pillars on page 56.	Markerboard, markers
✿ **Word Up (10–15 minutes)** **Preparation:** Print copies of the Word Up: Islam worksheet.	Word Up: Islam worksheet, pens or pencils
✿ **Sending Forth (5–10 minutes)**	Candle, matches or lighter

Don't Forget to ...

Whaddaya Know (or Think You Know)?

To begin, set out several sticky notes and pens. Invite the youth to write on the sticky notes any information they know (or think they know) about Islam. Suggest they also write any questions they have about Islam. Ask them to stick their notes on a markerboard or designated wall space.

> **You will need:** sticky notes and pens or pencils; if you have invited a guest expert, ask him or her to help with this activity.

When everyone has had an opportunity to contribute facts and questions, ask the youth to organize the sticky notes. First, ask them to set aside the questions. Then ask them to work together to arrange the facts into three categories: 1) pretty sure it's true, 2) think it might be true, and 3) really not sure if it's true.

If you have invited a Muslim person to speak to your group (see "Dialogue With an Expert" on page 61), ask him or her to look over the sticky notes and indicate which statements are true, which are true for some Muslims but not others, which are partially true, and which are completely false.

If you do not have an expert on hand, verify as many of the facts and answer as many questions as possible using the information on pages 52–57. Some of these facts and questions may also be covered in "The Truth Is Out There" (below).

Remind the youth that Islam, like Christianity and the other faiths we have studied, is a very diverse faith; that what is true for one Muslim might not be true for all Muslims; and that this session will focus on the beliefs and practices that most Muslims have in common.

The Truth Is Out There

List on a markerboard the following common statements about Islam, some of which are true and some of which are false:

> **You will need:** a markerboard and markers.

1. **Five times each day Muslims bow toward Mecca to pray.**

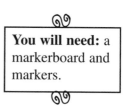

2. Jihad means "holy war" and is one of the Five Pillars of Islam.

3. All Muslim women are required to wear head scarves.

4. Muslims consider Jesus to be the last and greatest of the prophets.

5. Islam means "peace."

6. Muhammad is to Islam what Jesus is to Christianity.

7. Muslims trace their heritage back to Abraham.

For each statement ask the youth to vote "true" or "false." The answers are: 1. *True*; 2. *False—jihad is not one of the Five Pillars, and, while it sometimes involves war, jihad literally means "striving for the way of God"*; 3. *False—some movements in Islam do not require women to wear the head scarf or hijab*; 4. *False—they consider Muhammad the last and greatest of the prophets*; 5. *True—it also can mean "surrender" or "submission"*; 6. *False—while Muhammad is considered the greatest of the prophets, Muslims do not believe that he is the incarnation of God*; 7. *True—Muslims believe that the Arab people are descendants of Abraham's first son, Ishmael.*

Dialogue With an Expert

If possible invite a Muslim person from your community to explain to your youth the basics of his or her faith and to answer any questions that they have (such as those the youth wrote on the sticky notes).

> **You will need:** a guest expert on Islam.

Check out *burst.abingdonyouth.com* for a list of mosques in the United States. If there is not a mosque in your community, check the faculty of a nearby university for an expert on Islam. If your guest requests a list of topics to cover, give him or her a list of the key points on page 57.

The Word of God

If you invited a guest expert, he or she may assist with this activity by answering questions and offering correction and clarification.

You will need:
Bibles and recordings of recitations from the Quran. Optional: a copy of the Quran.

Hand out Bibles and ask a volunteer to read aloud **John 1:1-5** while remaining youth follow along. Say: "Christians believe that Jesus Christ is the Word of God and that we come to know God through Jesus Christ. Muslims have similar beliefs—not about the Prophet Muhammad but about the Quran."

Play some recordings of Quran recitation. (These are widely available on the Internet, see *burst.abingdonyouth.com* for more information.) If you have access to a copy of the Quran, pass it around and allow youth to look at it closely. As they are looking, ask the youth what they know about the Quran, the Muslim holy book. Interject the following points:

- Muslims believe that the Quran was written by God and that the Prophet Muhammad recorded God's exact words.

- The Quran is only properly read in Arabic, the language in which Muslims believe it was divinely revealed to Muhammad.

- Muslims believe that the Jewish and Christian Scriptures are revelations of God that have been corrupted by human translation and interpretation but that the words of the Quran are eternal and perfect.

- Because it is considered the Word of God, the Quran is a sacred relic for Muslims. It must not be destroyed or desecrated.

- The Quran is divided into 114 suras, or chapters. These chapters are arranged mostly by length, with longer suras toward the beginning and shorter ones toward the end.

As time permits, discuss ways in which the Quran is similar to and different from the Christian Bible.

Five Pillars

Challenge the youth, working individually or in small groups, to come up with one sentence each that summarizes what Christians believe. Give the youth a few minutes to work, then ask them to read aloud their sentences.

You will need: a markerboard, markers, and student books or copies of the Five Pillars of Islam handout.

Say: "The essence of Muslim belief can be summed up in a single sentence: 'There is no god but God, and Muhammad is His Prophet.' Repeating this statement, known as the Shahada, is one of the Five Pillars of Islam. The Five Pillars are the primary ways in which Muslims live out their faith."

Ask the youth to turn to page 19 of the student book or distribute copies of the Five Pillars of Islam handout (available at *burst. abingdonyouth.com*). Divide the youth into small groups, if possible separating the older (high school) youth from the younger (middle school) youth. Assign an adult leader to each small group. Instruct the groups to read about the Five Pillars and to discuss the following questions. (Write these questions on a markerboard.)

- **What do the Five Pillars tell us about a Muslim's relationship with God and others?** (Possible answers: *Fasting reminds Muslims that they are dependent on God; almsgiving reminds them of the importance of loving and serving others.*)

- **How might being faithful to these Five Pillars be difficult in our present-day culture?** (Possible answers: *Most schools and businesses don't break for noontime and mid-afternoon prayer; fasting can be difficult when one is bombarded with advertisements for snack foods.*)

- **In what ways are the Five Pillars similar to and different from Christian spiritual practices?** (Possible answers: *Repeating the Shahada and reciting the Apostles' Creed are both ways to affirm one's faith; almsgiving and tithing both involve faithful use of money; while some Christians make pilgrimages, there is not one sacred site to which most Christians travel.*)

Word Up

Hand out copies of the Word Up: Islam worksheet and explain that youth will take a look at some important terms and concepts associated with Islam. This handout is available at *burst.abingdonyouth.com*. Challenge youth, working individually or in teams, to match the terms to their correct definitions. The answers are:

> **You will need:** copies of the Word Up: Islam worksheet, pens or pencils.

Allah: the Arabic word for God

The Five Pillars of Islam: *shahada* (profession that "There is no god but God, and Muhammad is His Prophet); *salat* (prayer five times per day); *zakat* (almsgiving); *sawm* (fasting during the month of Ramadan); and *hajj* (pilgrimage to Mecca)

hadith: an account of the life and/or teaching of the Prophet Muhammad

hajj: a pilgrimage to Mecca and one of the Five Pillars of Islam. Muslims who are physically able and have the financial means are expected to make at least one pilgrimage to Mecca.

Ishmael: Abraham's son by Sarah's servant Hagar. Muslims believe that he is the father of the Arab people.

Kaaba: literally means "cube"; a cube-shaped building located in Mecca; built, according to Muslims, by Abraham and Ishmael. Muslims face in its direction when they pray.

Mecca: the sacred city in which Muhammad was born and to which Muslims are expected to make pilgrimages

mosque: a Muslim place of worship

Ramadan: the ninth month of the Muslim year and the month during which the Quran was first revealed to Muhammad; a sacred month of fasting

salat: praying five times each day facing Mecca; one of the Five Pillars of Islam

sawm: the practice of fasting during the month of Ramadan; one of the Five Pillars of Islam

sharia: Islamic law

Shia: the second largest sect of Islam; believes that Muhammad appointed his son-in-law Ali as his successor

sunna: the words, actions, and example of the Prophet Muhammad

Sunni: the popular name for the largest sect of Islam

sura: a chapter of the Quran; there are 114 chapters.

umma: the Muslim community

zakat: giving alms for the benefit of the poor and needy; one of the Five Pillars of Islam

Sending Forth

Gather the youth in a circle, dim the lights, and light a candle. Say: "Today we learned some of the basics of Islam, including the Five Pillars of Islam. The Five Pillars are instructions to Muslims for living faithful lives. To close I want you to think of some of the 'pillars' of Christianity. What sorts of things should Christians do to live faithful lives?"

> **You will need:** a candle and matches.

Pass the candle around the circle. Invite each person, when he or she is holding the candle, to name one important Christian practice or discipline. Then close in prayer, reaffirming the essentials of the Christian faith and thanking God for the opportunity to learn about other faith traditions.

BRINGING IT ALL TOGETHER

*In everything do to others as you
would have them do to you; for this is the
law and the prophets.*
—Matthew 7:12

Getting Ready

While there is value in learning about and better understanding the history, beliefs, and practices of the world's great faith traditions, it is also important that we, as Christians, take time to reflect on what makes our tradition unique and why we call ourselves followers of Christ.

Throughout this study, youth have explored some of the essentials of Hinduism, Buddhism, Judaism, and Islam. In this session you will help them identify some of the essentials of Christianity. As Christians, what is our story? What basic beliefs do all (or most) Christians hold in common? What role does the Bible play in our faith tradition? How do Christians follow the teachings of Jesus and live as disciples of Christ?

The purpose of this final session is not to compare and contrast Christianity and other faiths (though you will do a bit of that). Instead the main purpose is to help youth gain some idea of what to say and/or do when someone asks, "Why are you a Christian?" or "What do you believe?" or "What do Christians do?"

✽ Food Ideas

Since this is the final session in this study, consider serving fun snacks such as popcorn, chips, and cookies. Be sure to also provide some healthy options such as fruit or vegetables.

✽ Music Ideas

As a celebration of your Christian faith, consider playing or singing some favorite hymns and/or praise songs.

Getting Ready: This session's purpose is to help youth gain some idea of what to say and/or do when someone asks, "Why are you a Christian?" or "What do you believe?" Think about your personal answers to these questions. Also review the following activities and gather or prepare needed supplies.

ACTIVITIES	SUPPLIES
🌀 **What We Have in Common (10 minutes)** Preparation: Review basics of the four faith traditions.	Markerboard, markers
🌀 **The Pursuit of Goodness (10 minutes)** Preparation: Review the four faith traditions' emphases on pursuing goodess and morality.	Bibles
🌀 **Dialogue With an Expert (15–20 minutes)** Preparation: Invite a guest expert on Christianity.	
🌀 **They'll Know We Are Christians (10 minutes)** Preparation: Read the Scriptures on page 71.	Bibles
🌀 **Word Up (15–20 minutes)**	Paper, pens or pencils, access to a photocopier (or slips of paper, and a bag or box or hat)
🌀 **Sending Forth (5–10 minutes)**	Candle, matches or lighter

Don't Forget to . . .

What We Have in Common

To begin, ask the youth to recall the four faith traditions they have learned about: Hinduism, Buddhism, Judaism, and Islam. Briefly review each religion, asking the following questions:

> **You will need:** a markerboard and markers.

- What do you know about the story of this faith tradition?

- What are some of this religion's core beliefs?

- What books and writings are sacred in this tradition?

- What rituals and practices do persons in this tradition observe?

After you've reviewed each religion, ask the same set of questions about Christianity. The answers youth give about Chistianity likely will be lengthy and will reflect a wide variety of perspectives. Use this opportunity to point out the diversity and complexity of Christian beliefs and traditions and to tell youth that if a group of Hindus or Muslims were to answer these same questions about their faith the answers probably would be just as lengthy and varied.

Now divide the youth into small groups of three or four. Ask each group to compile a list of characteristics that these faith traditions have in common. They might note that Christianity, Islam, and Judaism all trace their heritage back to Abraham; that both Hinduism and Buddhism developed in India and involve escaping from samsara; or that all five traditions have something to say about goodness and morality. Give the youth a few minutes to work, then ask someone from each group to read aloud his or her group's examples. As each group reports, list on a markerboard those items that any or all of the religions you studied have in common with Christianity.

Say: "We must be careful when we compare religions. For example, while it is true that all of the faith traditions we've studied have sacred books and writings, it is also true that the Muslim understanding of the Quran is different from the Christian understanding of the Bible or the Hindu understanding of the Bhagavad Gita. And if we try to compare the Christian belief in resurrection to the Buddhist belief in nirvana, we lose sight of the unique meaning of both concepts. Still, it is good to be able to point to similar beliefs and to know that we're all seeking a better and more fulfilling life for all people."

The Pursuit of Goodness

Say: "One of the elements that Christianity has in common with the religions we've studied is an emphasis on pursuing goodness and morality. The Buddhist standards for morality are the Eightfold Path and the Five Precepts. Muslims have the Five Pillars of Islam, which involve ethical behavior and compassion for others as well as personal devotion to God. Hindus believe in good works as a way to earn good karma. And Jews observe the mitzvot, or commandments, in the Torah."

> **You will need:**
> Bibles.

Divide the youth into age-specific small groups. Ask the groups to discuss the following questions:

- As Christians, what are our standards of morality? How do we know what is right, what is wrong, and what God wants us to do?

- Why, or how, are good works important to us as Christians? (Encourage the groups to read Scriptures such as **Romans 3:27-28**; **Galatians 5:22-26**; and **James 2:14-26** as they discuss this question.)

- As Christians, how does God expect us to treat others?

Give the groups several minutes to discuss the questions, then invite each group to summarize its answers. Ask a volunteer to read aloud **Matthew 25:31-40**. Say: "In this Scripture, Jesus is clear that he expects us to show others love, hospitality, and compassion. All of the other faith traditions we've learned about also value acts of love, hospitality, and compassion, though different religions stress good deeds for different reasons."

Dialogue With an Expert

Keeping with the pattern of inviting an expert to talk about each of the religions you study, invite an expert on Christianity to answer youths' questions about Christian theology, Scripture, and practice. Your expert might be

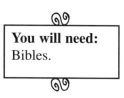

You will need: a guest expert on Christianity.

your senior pastor, a member of your pastoral staff, or a professor from a nearby seminary or university. (Or you might consider yourself an expert.) It may seem unusual to invite an expert to answer questions about Christianity when your youth already have weekly opportunities to learn about their faith (in worship, Sunday school, youth group, and so on), but even the most active, church-going teens have questions about Christian doctrine and what the Bible teaches. Youth need permission to ask and struggle with these questions in a safe and nonthreatening environment.

They'll Know We Are Christians

Say: "All of the faith traditions we have studied have an affect on what people believe, what they value, and how they act. Religion sometimes places people at odds with the culture in which they live or compels them to

You will need: Bibles.

live in ways different from the people around them. In other words, religion has a way of setting people apart."

Ask the youth to think of ways in which people set themselves apart in each of the four faith traditions you have studied. Examples may include: Hindus practicing yoga; Buddhists following the Eightfold Path and the Five Precepts; Jews keeping kosher and observing Shabbat; and Muslims praying five times each day facing Mecca (salat).

Say: "As Christians, we also should set ourselves apart." Ask:

- How do you set yourself apart as a Christian?

- How might someone recognize you as a Christian?

Ask volunteers to read aloud the following Scriptures and talk about what each Scripture has to say about how we as Christians set ourselves apart. (If you wish, add other relevant Scriptures.)

- **Matthew 5:43-48**

- **Matthew 28:18-20**

- **Romans 12:9-18**

- **Colossians 3:12-17**

- **1 Thessalonians 5:14-22**

- **James 5:13-16**

- **1 Peter 2:9**

Word Up

As a part of each previous session, you have challenged youth to match key terms and concepts to the correct descriptions or definitions. In this session the youth will design the activity.

> **You will need:** paper, pens or pencils, and a photocopier OR slips of paper, and a bag or box or hat.

Divide the youth into groups of three of four each and hand out paper and pens. Challenge each group to design a quiz in which one must match important Christian terms and concepts to the correct descriptions or definitions. Encourage the groups to include between ten and fifteen terms and concepts that they think are essential to understanding Christianity. (Examples would include: *Christ, Holy Spirit, grace, atonement, salvation,* and *church*.)

Give the groups several minutes to work. As they work, walk around the room and make yourself available to answer questions or to help define words. (If you have several adult helpers, assign one to each group for this purpose.)

After the groups have finished creating their quizzes, collect and photocopy them. While you are making copies (or you might ask another helper to make the copies), ask the youth to talk about why this activity was challenging. Then hand out copies of each group's quizzes to one of the other groups. (For example, give copies of Group 1's quiz to Group 2, copies of Group 2's quiz to Group 3, and so on.)

Give the youth a few minutes to complete the quizzes, then ask a member of each group to reveal the correct answers to his or her group's quiz. Ask:

- How difficult were these quizzes to create? to answer?

- Do you disagree with or have questions about any definitions on the quiz you took?

Option: Instead of asking youth to create quizzes, instruct each youth to write on separate slips of paper two or three important Christian terms or concepts. Collect the slips in a hat, bag, or box. Divide the youth into two teams and, using the terms or concepts youth have provided, play either charades or a variation on Pictionary.™

Sending Forth

Gather youth in a circle, dim the lights, and light a candle. Invite the youth to spend a moment in silence reflecting on what they have learned during this study about Hinduism, Buddhism, Judaism, Islam, and about the Christian faith.

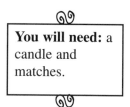

You will need: a candle and matches.

Go around the circle and give each person an opportunity to name one fact about Hinduism, Buddhism, Judaism, or Islam and a new fact that he or she learned about Christianity. Close in prayer, thanking God for the opportunity to come together as a community of believers to grow in faith and to learn about the beliefs and traditions of others.

ADDITIONAL RESOURCES

Church Statements

Below are several statements from Christian denominations regarding Christians' relationships with people of other faiths.

The United Methodist Church

Rights of Religious Minorities—Religious persecution has been common in the history of civilization. We urge policies and practices that ensure the right of every religious group to exercise its faith free from legal, political, or economic restrictions. We condemn all overt and covert forms of religious intolerance, being especially sensitive to their expression in media stereotyping. We assert the right of all religions and their adherents to freedom from legal, economic, and social discrimination.

—From "The Social Principles of The United Methodist Church" from *The Book of Discipline of The United Methodist Church, 2008*. Copyright © 2008 by The United Methodist Publishing House; ¶162, page 109. Used by permission.

The intent in developing interreligious relationships is not to amalgamate all faiths into one religion. ... To engage in interreligious dialogue is neither to endorse nor to deny the faith of other people. In dialogue we seek insight into the wisdom of other traditions and we hope to overcome our fears and misapprehensions about them. Far from requiring a lessening of commitment to Christ, effective dialogue is only possible when one's own faith is strong, and may ultimately serve to deepen or extend it.

—From "Called to Be Neighbors and Witnesses: Guidelines for Interreligious Relationships," *The Book of Resolutions of The United Methodist Church, 2008*. Copyright © 2008 by The United Methodist Publishing House; page 288. Used by permission.

Presbyterian Church (USA)

We are called to work with others in our pluralistic societies for the well-being of our world and for justice, peace, and the sustainability of creation. We do so in the faith that, through God's spirit, the Church is a sign and means of God's intention for the wholeness and unity of humankind and of all creation. . . .

—From Presbyterian Principles for Interfaith Dialogue, Part 3. Used by permission.

As much as I can, [with people of other religions] I should meet friendship with friendship, hostility with kindness, generosity with gratitude, persecution with forbearance, truth with agreement, and error with truth. I should express my faith with humility and devotion as the occasion requires, whether silently or openly, boldly or meekly, by word or by deed. I should avoid compromising the truth on the one hand and being narrow-minded on the other. In short, I should always welcome and accept these others in a way that honors and reflects the Lord's welcome and acceptance of me.

The limits to salvation, whatever they may be, are known only to God. Three truths above all are certain. God is a holy God who is not to be trifled with. No one will be saved except by grace alone. And no judge could possibly be more gracious than our Lord and Savior, Jesus Christ.

—From Presbyterian Study Catechism (Questions 52 and 49).
Used by permission.

The Episcopal Church

This Conference commends dialogue with people of other faiths as a part of Christian discipleship and mission, with the understanding that:

(1) dialogue begins when people meet each other; (2) dialogue depends upon mutual understanding, mutual respect and mutual trust; (3) dialogue makes it possible to share in service to the community; (4) dialogue becomes a medium of authentic witness.

—From the 1988 Lambeth Conference, Resolution 20; Used by permission, the Secretary General of the Anglican Communion 2006.

The Roman Catholic Church

[In] Hinduism, men contemplate the divine mystery and express it through an inexhaustible abundance of myths and through searching philosophical inquiry. They seek freedom from the anguish of our human condition either through ascetical practices or profound meditation or a flight to God with love and trust. Again, Buddhism, in its various forms, realizes the radical insufficiency of this changeable world; it teaches a way by which men, in a devout and confident spirit, may be able either to acquire the state of perfect liberation, or attain, by their own efforts or through higher help, supreme illumination. Likewise, other religions found everywhere try to counter the restlessness of the human heart, each in its own manner, by proposing "ways," comprising teachings, rules of life, and sacred rites. The Catholic Church rejects nothing that is true and holy in these religions. She regards with sincere reverence those ways of conduct and of life, those precepts and teachings which, though differing in many aspects from the ones she holds and sets forth, nonetheless often reflect a ray of that Truth which enlightens all men. Indeed, she proclaims, and ever must proclaim Christ "the way, the truth, and the life" (John 14:6), in whom men may find the fullness of religious life, in whom God has reconciled all things to Himself....

The Church regards with esteem also the [Muslims]. They adore the one God, living and subsisting in Himself; merciful and all-powerful, the Creator of heaven and earth, who has spoken to men; they take pains to submit wholeheartedly to even His inscrutable decrees, just as Abraham, with whom the faith of Islam takes pleasure in linking itself, submitted to God....

The Church of Christ acknowledges that, according to God's saving design, the beginnings of her faith and her election are found already among the Patriarchs, Moses and the prophets. ...The Church, therefore, cannot forget that she received the revelation of the Old Testament through the people with whom God in His inexpressible mercy concluded the Ancient Covenant. Nor can she forget that she draws sustenance from the root of that well-cultivated olive tree onto which have been grafted the wild shoots, the Gentiles. Indeed, the Church believes that by His cross Christ, Our Peace, reconciled Jews and Gentiles. making both one in Himself.

—From "Declaration on the Relation of the Church to Non-Christian Religions,"
Proclaimed by Pope Paul VI, October 28, 1965.

Images of Hindu Deities

On the following pages are images of a few of the many deities recognized and revered in the Hindu tradition. You may reproduce these images for the "Deity I.D." activity on pages 19–21.

Brahma

Shiva

Vishnu

Parvati as Durga

Lakshmi

Saraswati

Ganesh

Other World Religion Resources

Books

Christianity and World Religions: Wrestling With Questions People Ask, by Adam Hamilton (Nashville: Abingdon Press, 2005). ISBN: 9780687494309.

A History of the World's Religions, twelfth edition, by David S. Noss (New Jersey: Prentice Hall, 2007). ISBN: 9780136149842.

How to Be a Perfect Stranger: The Essential Religious Etiquette Handbook, second edition, Stuart Matlins and Arthur Magida, eds. (Woodstock, VT: SkyLight Paths Publishing, 2006). ISBN: 978159473140.

Understanding Other Religious Worlds: A Guide to Interreligious Education, by Judith Berling (Maryknoll, NY: Orbis, 2004). ISBN: 9781570755163.

World Religions in America, fourth edition, Jacob Neusner, ed. (Louisville: Westminster John Knox Press, 2009). ISBN: 9780664233204.

World Religions Today, by John Esposito, Darrell Fasching, and Todd Lewis (New York: Oxford University Press, 2002). ISBN: 9780195176995.

The World's Religions, by Huston Smith (New York: Harper Collins, 1991). ISBN: 9780062508119.

The World's Wisdom: Sacred Texts of the World's Religions, by Philip Novak (New York: Harper Collins, 1995). ISBN: 9780060663421.

Video Viewing Note: When you show home videocassettes or DVDs to a group of learners, you need to obtain a license. You can get a public performance license from Christian Video Licensing International (1-888-771-2854, cvli.com). The license can cost over $100. Check with your church to see whether an umbrella license has already been obtained. Through conferences, jurisdictions, dioceses, and other structures, many denominations secure licenses for their churches to show films.

Relevant Websites

Beliefnet
www.beliefnet.com
Beliefnet provides a wealth of information, commentary, prayers, and inspirational materials related to all the world's major religions.

BuddhaNet
www.buddhanet.net
BuddaNet describes itself as the "Worldwide Buddhist Information and Education Network."

Hindunet: The Hindu Universe
www.hindunet.org
Hindunet offers a wide variety of news and information pertaining to Hinduism.

Islam.com
www.islam.com
Islam.com is web portal that strives to provide fair and accurate information and resources for and about the worldwide Muslim community.

Judaism 101
www.jewfaq.org
From the website: "Judaism 101 is an online encyclopedia of Judaism, covering Jewish beliefs, people, places, things, language, scripture, holidays, practices, and customs."

Pew Forum: Religion in American Culture
religions.pewforum.org
Pew Forum's Religion in American Culture website provides facts, figures, charts, and maps that illustrate Americans' beliefs, values, and religious affiliations.

NOTE: At the time of publication, all websites were correct and operational.